An Employee's Guide to Stock Options

An Employee's Guide to Stock Options

Beth V. Walker, CRPC

McGraw-Hill

New York Chicago San Francisco Lisbon
London Madrid Mexico City Milan New Delhi
San Juan Seoul Singapore Sydney Toronto

The **McGraw·Hill** Companies

1 2 3 4 5 6 7 8 9 0 DOC/DOC 0 9 8 7 6 5 4 3

ISBN 0-07-140230-6

Printed and bound by RR Donnelley

This book is printed on recycled, acid-free paper containing a minimum of 50% recycled de-inked paper.

CONTENTS

FOREWORD

Over 10 million Americans have employee stock options, but only a few understand and know how to manage this valuable resource. I've met chief executive officers who do not know the difference between a qualified and a nonqualified stock option, and I've heard about company presidents who lost millions of dollars because they did not protect the value of their vested options.

An Employee's Guide to Stock Options can help employees and executives in American companies preserve hundreds of millions of dollars of net worth. While other books have been written about employee stock options, some promote only one style of options management or exercise and others are so technical that few readers can comprehend them.

An Employee's Guide to Stock Options is a delightful and much needed contribution to our understanding of the most important employee incentive of all. In this book financial planner Beth Walker uses an entertaining writing style to educate the reader about the intricacies of nonqualified stock options (NQSOs), incentive stock options (ISOs), employee stock purchase plans (ESPPs), and restricted stock plans (RSPs). She also helps the reader determine how much his or her options are worth and what taxes will be owed upon exercising them. This remarkable book is both comprehensive and engaging.

I am a compensation and options researcher, and one of my special areas of interest and expertise is the protection of employee stock options (ESOs). Few executives or employees know that it is possible to protect vested stock options. In fact, I can think of no other book on the subject that mentions it. Beth Walker shows how to use powerful protection techniques that once were reserved for only the highest-level executives who could afford the best (and most expensive) advisers. These techniques alone could help some readers of the book preserve hundreds of thousands to millions of dollars of their net worth.

Her treatment of the tax issues involved in exercising stock options could save readers tens of thousands of dollars or more in state and federal taxes.

The need for education about employee stock options is critical. Collectively, employees of American companies have lost hundreds of billions of dollars of their net worth because of a lack of understanding of how to protect their stock options, when and how to exercise them, and how to manage the tax issues involved in exercising options. While companies spend billions of dollars every year on educational programs and seminars on every subject imaginable, almost nothing is spent to educate employees about their stock options. The sad result is that options holders have lost hundreds of billions of dollars that they could have spent on homes, cars, college educations, and vacations and to fund retirement programs or could have used to start and grow new businesses. This book will provide employees the knowledge they need to intelligently manage what could be their most valuable asset. This is a book that every human resources director should hand out to every employee who receives stock options.

I spend more than 50 percent of my time training and consulting with financial planners, stockbrokers, pension fund managers, and other financial professionals, and I write for several of the most prominent financial adviser websites. In doing my consulting and public speaking work, I have met several thousand financial planners over the last decade. I would estimate that fewer than 1 percent of all financial advisers or stockbrokers understand employee stock options. Beth Walker is one of those rare financial planners who has a deep understanding of this prized asset, and now millions of Americans will be able to avail themselves of her wisdom.

As a result of mismanagement of employee stock options and the staggering losses suffered by options holders, a record number of lawsuits have been filed by top attorneys such as Lawrence Klayman. Companies and financial advisers who use the knowledge contained in this book will be able to serve their employees and clients better and avoid the huge settlements and judgments that are being handed down.

It is my hope that *An Employee's Guide to Stock Options* will become one of the most widely read books in the field and that employers finally will realize their fiduciary duty to provide some education and training on how to manage and protect the value of employee stock options. As an expert witness, I am keenly aware of the fact that sometimes litigation is necessary to bring about needed reforms. However, even better than litigation to recover losses is education to prevent losses. The education provided by Beth Walker in this book is priceless.

For all these reasons, *An Employee's Guide to Stock Options* is a book I can wholeheartedly recommend to the 10 million Americans who have employee stock options and to the thousands of companies that offer stock options to their employees.

Dr. Donald Moine, President of
The Association of Human
Achievement, Inc.
DrMoine@aol.com

PREFACE

According to the National Center for Employee Ownership, during the 1990s the number of employees getting stock options ballooned from less than 1 million at the start of the decade to about 10 million by the end. The press was full of reports of "optionaires," employees who struck it rich when their company's stock skyrocketed. Then the market collapsed, and stories were written about option tax disasters, precipitous declines in morale among option-ladened employees, and a rapid move away from compensating employees with equity. While much of the reporting on stock options was accurate and insightful, much of it subscribed to common myths that distorted what was happening both during the market's rise and after its fall. For a variety of reasons, options granted to most or all employees have become an institutionalized part of compensation at many companies.

But although options have become ubiquitous, their development as a broad-based compensation strategy is still in its infancy. It's no surprise, therefore, that few employees, even highly compensated ones, understand how to use their options wisely. A distressing number allow their options to expire even when they are "in the money." Thus, employees voluntarily have given up the right to buy stock for less—often much less—than its market value because they didn't know the rules, weren't paying attention, or "just didn't get around to it." More commonly, employees get caught in avoidable tax traps that can end up costing them more than they made on their options or fail to plan when they exercise their options to get the maximum value out of them. When you consider how much time and effort people make to save a few dollars on a pair of socks, $100 on a new television, or even a few thousand on a new car, it's amazing to realize that they spend little or no time thinking about how to maximize their gains from options that can be worth tens or hundreds of thousands of dollars or even more.

This book helps employees make much better use of their options. It's not a detailed work about option rules; it's a sensible call for employees to set up some basic guidelines about how to think about their options and get help in using them wisely. It's encouraging to see these kinds of resources becoming available, because the option concept is here to stay.

There are a lot of myths about options. When you understand how wrong these myths are, the importance of resources like these becomes apparent.

Myth 1: Most People Who Get Options Worked for Dot-Coms

One of the most prevalent and misleading misperceptions was (and still is) that most employees who get options worked (or now work) for dot-com companies, most of which were small, pre-initial public offering (IPO) ventures. This was never even close to true. There were a lot of dot coms, to be sure, and most of them did give most or all their employees options, but most employed well under 100 people. The total employment at all the pre-IPO dot-com companies never amounted to more than a few percent of the 10 million people getting options. In fact, almost all the employees getting options work (and worked) for publicly traded companies, and most of them work for large employers. Verizon, for instance, makes most of its over 200,000 employees eligible for options. It would take 5,000 dot coms with 40 employees each to have that many employees.

Myth 2: Well at Least They Worked for High-Technology Companies

The large majority of high-technology companies make most of their employees eligible for stock options, but even the highest estimates for the technology sector place employment at about 5 million. If 60 percent of these employees get options (a reasonable guess), only 3 million employees getting options are technology workers. In fact, about 15 to 20 percent of all public companies give employees options, and many of these companies are outside the technology sector. Many large banks provide broad options, for instance, as do a number of large pharmaceutical companies. Retailers such as Whole Foods, Walgreens, and Starbucks give out broad options. So do PepsiCo and Procter & Gamble.

Myth 3: Most People Give Up Pay to Get Options

Economists tell us there is no free lunch, and so if employees get options they must be giving up pay or benefits. To be sure, some employees have done just that. Lots of people were lured to start-up companies at low salaries in return for substantial option packages, but these people are the exceptions. For the most part they are at the managerial level or higher or are people with special skills, such as programmers. Altogether, they constitute only a tiny proportion of all the employees getting options. Data from Professors Joseph Blasi and Douglas Kruse at Rutgers University indicate that overall, employees who get options are paid about 7 percent more in wages than are comparable employees in comparable companies that do not give out options. The fact is that with a tight labor market—and we still have a labor market that is tighter than historical standards—it is very difficult to lure all but a handful of risk takers to jobs whose base pay and benefits are not comparable to what could be earned elsewhere. Options are gravy that helps companies distinguish themselves. In the tech sector they are not even that: Everyone gives out options widely, and so they are just part of the ante to the game.

Myth 4: Options Are Worthwhile Only if Your Company Is Publicly Traded

Many stories advised employees that if their company was not on a public stock market, their options were worthless and would be until the company did an IPO, which very few ever would do. In fact, most closely held companies giving out options are sold (assuming they don't close first), at which time the options usually are exchanged for cash or for stock in the acquiring company at the sale price.

Myth 5: Options Are the Last Decade's Compensation

Surely, this myth goes, no one wants options anymore. Lots of employees have lots of options deeply "underwater," meaning that the price at which the employee can buy shares is way above the current price, probably making the option worthless. So who wants more? Employees do, and employers want employees to have them. Data from the National Center for Employee Ownership show that most companies with broad-based stock options plans have no plans to change, much less eliminate them. Most of these companies now dole out the options over a period of years rather than all at once. Thus, employees got some options at a very high price but will get more at what seems like a very low one. These new options could be worth a lot one day. Moreover, many employees have options in companies that have been more stable, and their options are still worth something or are close to that point.

To be sure, people and companies are now more realistic about what options can mean. They probably are not going to make more than a handful of people rich, but for most holders, they provide a worthwhile additional benefit. And for most option-granting companies they provide a way to link employee and corporate fortunes for the long term. Options are not the ready path to riches they may have seemed to some or the magic elixir for corporate recruitment, retention, and motivation problems they seemed to others, but they have too many advantages to both sides to go the way of hula hoops and pet rocks.

Corey Rosen is executive director of the National Center for Employee Ownership (NCEO), a private, nonprofit membership, information, and research organization in Oakland, CA. For more information about the NCEO, as well as its research, books, seminars, and member services, go to www.nceo.org.

ACKNOWLEDGMENTS

My thirst for knowledge regarding equity compensation and any wisdom that may result from that quest has been a lifelong pursuit. Along the way, however, I have encountered and will continue to encounter many teachers and mentors.

I'd like to thank Ken Parker for creating the National Institute for Estate Planners and providing me with an excellent forum for developing the Optioneering® concept. His enthusiasm and passion for comprehensive estate planning are contagious, and his commitment to educating the financial services industry is to be commended.

I'd like to thank the folks at Net Worth Strategies, Inc., Sarah Ward, Bill Dillhoefer and Bill Briggs, in particular. Having created some of the best tools I've seen for modeling the consequences of stock option compensation and having combined those great resources with a "can do" company culture, they are leading the financial services industry in terms of tackling this complicated planning area.

Many thanks go to my brilliant partners—Robert Williams, Lisa Wright, Cheryl Constantino, and Don Parker—for their patience, understanding, and support of my efforts to complete this book. Their generosity of time, talent, and expertise is much appreciated. Thanks also to Jennifer Caligiuri, whose friendship, loyalty, hard work, and sense of humor make life easier and more enjoyable every day.

The creative genius and artistic integrity of my brother, Dr. Robert Vivian, are responsible for this book being published in the first place. It was Bob who introduced me to Meredith Phelan, and Meredith who championed my work with such enthusiasm that McGraw-Hill decided to take a chance on an unknown, first-time author. I thank Kelli Christiansen and her team at McGraw-Hill's Professional Book Group for sharing my vision of this project and their enthusiasm for bringing it to life.

Finally, I thank my husband, Derek, for his support, kindness, and patience. Most of all, I thank him for sitting next to me on that United flight from Vancouver, B.C., to Chicago in 1996 and making the call to say hi a few days later. Lucky me!

INTRODUCTION

Stock options: We know we want them and are glad we have them, but does anyone really know what we're supposed to do with them?

Stock option compensation is a strong currency in today's economy, but it's hard to buy groceries, pay the mortgage, or put one's child through school with what is essentially paper wealth. In Las Vegas terms, the vast majority of today's "optionaires" have no idea how or when to take their chips off the table and go home a winner.

With an estimated 10 million U.S. employees receiving some form of stock options, what began as the ultimate executive perk has evolved into a ubiquitous incentive for every equity culture that can defend its business model. Companies that have to compete for the truly talented in today's labor market have learned to leverage stock option compensation to attract and retain the skilled employees required at every level of the organization.

Administrative assistants, help desk personnel, consultants, marketing executives, chief executive officers (CEOs), chief financial officers (CFOs), attorneys, and even celebrities have traded cash for the potential to experience the adrenaline rush of wealth resulting from stock options. Some, sadly, have felt the unforgiving blow that equity compensation can wield upon the unsuspecting. Regardless of our role in today's workplace, we are simply not equipped to manage the complex compensation tool that masquerades under the simple term *stock options*. We resemble a 16-year-old with a new driver's license: We are fumbling for the keys and promising to be in before our curfew as the Space Shuttle awaits us in the driveway.

The financial services industry for the most part simply isn't prepared. Only a handful of advisers even attempt to position themselves as experts in the area of employee stock option planning. Many stockbrokers, certified public accountants (CPAs), and attorneys claim they can assist us in deciphering the confusing vocabulary and complicated tax consequences associated with this form of compensation, but few actually know what they are doing. There are qualified professionals who can assist us in managing our equity compensation, but finding them takes both time and money and a critical eye for talent and expertise.

Employee stock options force most of us into a scenario we've managed to put off as long as possible: formal financial planning. We never really thought we needed it, or we've been putting it off until it was absolutely necessary. We're educated, we're gainfully employed in a company we hope has a bright future, and we're putting money into our 401k plans. We're handling things ourselves, we've weathered the latest downturn in the markets, and we're feeling pretty good about our financial future.

Besides, the prospect of disclosing the intimate details of our personal finances to someone and trusting that person to "do right by us" is a little too scary.

My name is Beth V. Walker, and I resemble these remarks.

I worked in corporate America in the 1980s and early 1990s and earned my share of stock options. I made the classic mistakes associated with using one of my stockbrokers as a financial strategist and learned how expensive ignorance can be. My first experience exercising and selling my employee stock options left me feeling frustrated, angry, and embarrassed. I was frustrated because my expectations (in terms of how much money would go into my bank account) were unrealistic and therefore unmet; I was angry because it seemed that my company and my broker never really cared whether I understood the process; I was embarrassed because I considered myself financially savvy and didn't want to admit I had no idea what I was doing.

My circuitous career path introduced me to the concept of equity compensation and eventually led me into the financial services industry, where I've found my true calling. Having been reintroduced to the complexities of stock options from a financial planning perspective, I am now in the business of helping people avoid the painful, frustrating, and expensive experiences I went through as an employee on the receiving end of what should be considered a reward for a job well done. I am a financial consultant specializing in the area of advanced financial planning associated with employee stock option compensation.

And it is, literally, a labor of love.

It's *labor* in that every individual's stock option scenario comes with its own unique challenges: It doesn't fit into a formula or pre-packaged program. Each client's situation requires a willingness to entertain multiple strategies and change tactics in midstream, the use of complex (and many times new) modeling tools, and the co-operation of a team of advisers of the type that is usually reserved for sophisticated estate planning.

It's *love* in that my husband, Derek, unintentionally introduced me to the most explosive, complicated, and rewarding area of financial services being practiced. When the software company Derek worked for announced it was going public, I began to investigate the tools and resources available to us for our personal financial planning situation. I was shocked to find that very few resources or knowledgeable advisers existed—a startling realization for a professional in the business of full-service financial planning! My own miserable experience resurfaced, and I vowed at that moment to do something about it.

The harder I looked, the less confident I was that my professional peers could provide comprehensive financial solutions related to our personal goals. Many of the resources I tapped provided me with contradictory opinions regarding option exercise strategies, tax consequences, and diversification alternatives. The attorneys, CPAs, and other financial advisers I spoke with had very limited experience with stock option clients, and not one of them had personally received stock option compensation. They couldn't appreciate the emotional, as well as financial, consequences of managing our stock options and simply didn't have our sense of urgency in terms of developing that expertise any time soon.

Stock options revealed themselves to me as "stealth wealth" in every sense of the phrase.

Richard Bach, in his book *Illusions*, wrote that you teach best what you most need to learn; I have taken his words to heart. I have immersed myself in the details related to stock option compensation, refocused my financial planning practice, partnered with some exceptional advisers who provide expertise in areas that complement my own, and dedicated myself to providing comprehensive wealth management for those who have received and will continue to receive stock option compensation. Employee stock options represent the greatest wealth-building opportunity most employees will ever experience, and I am committed to helping successful professionals in many industry sectors pocket more of what they've earned.

In the chapters ahead we'll answer questions such as "What is a stock option?" "When should I exercise my options?" "What are the tax consequences related to my equity compensation?" "How do I keep more of what I've earned?" and "Who can I turn to for advice?"

My goal in writing this book is very simple: to provide you with the information and tools necessary for making educated decisions regarding your stock option compensation. At the end of the day it's not what you make, it's what you keep.

1

A STOCK OPTION IS JUST LIKE SEX

The purpose of this chapter is to explain in simple terms what a stock option is, why it can be valuable to an employee receiving it as part of their overall compensation package, and what types of questions should be prompted by an equity compensation award.

Why do so many smart and successful professionals make such expensive mistakes when it comes to handling their stock option compensation? *Because a stock option is just like sex.*

Everybody wants some, everybody claims to know how to do it, and everybody makes a mistake the first time he or she tries it.

Do you remember how you first learned about "the birds and the bees"? It wasn't your parents; they were too embarrassed to discuss it with you because their parents never talked to them about it. You probably learned it from that one kid who always seemed to be a few steps ahead of the crowd. Of course, as the facts fell into place and you were able to piece together some reliable information, you developed your own sense of how things worked, ultimately learning by trial and error.

Welcome to the most common approach to managing the currency of today's workplace.

Stock options, like parenting and marriage and sex, fall into that category of really important things we're never educated about.

1

Sure, your company will provide you with plan documents and exercise forms and refer you to a tax adviser or stockbroker, but they don't really want to get involved in how you handle your equity compensation. They aren't licensed to provide you with investment and/or tax advice, and they'll never take on that liability. Besides, you're a successful professional—a potential owner, for goodness' sake! You of all people don't need to be told what to do with your options. And you, being the bright, above-average individual who was awarded these options, aren't going to admit that you have no idea what to do with them.

> The stock option is one of the trickiest assets to handle because of the complexity of tax and regulatory issues.
>
> Source: "Wall Street's Bum Steer on Options," *Investment News*, Vol. 6, No. 12, March 25, 2002.

Don't let one of the greatest wealth-building tools you will encounter in your working lifetime slide off your personal balance sheet because of ignorance. Learning what you really have and how you can keep more of it is worth every minute and dollar you invest in the process.

What Is a Stock Option, and Why Should You Care?

If you're getting stock options, you're happy about it—or you should be—but you may not be exactly sure what they are or what they're worth.

The idea is actually quite simple.

A stock option gives you the opportunity, but not the obligation, to purchase a certain number of shares in your company, at a fixed price, for a certain number of years in the future no matter how much the market price of the stock fluctuates.

This price usually is referred to as the *grant price* but is also called the *exercise* or *strike price*. That price is almost always the fair market value (meaning the price point at which a public company's stock trades for on an exchange such as the New York Stock Exchange or NASDAQ) of your company's stock on the day the award is made.

Since options give you, by contractual agreement, the right to purchase stock at a certain price within a certain time frame, an option becomes only valuable if the stock price increases.

If the price does increase, you can buy the shares at the lower grant price and sell them at the higher current market value price. If the price does not increase, you can choose *not* to exercise your option to buy the stock before the expiration date (not to be confused with the earlier vesting date), basically letting your options expire.

The true value of a stock option is the potential for appreciation in the price of the stock without the investment risk.

If you have everything to gain and nothing to lose, why would your company make these options available to you? What's in it for them?

Historically, stock options were awarded almost exclusively to the board of directors, top management or "key" employees, and consultants to motivate their performance and link their financial interests to those of the company and its shareholders.

But as the industrial age has given way to the knowledge economy, many companies have come to recognize that the only sustainable competitive advantage they have is their people. Essentially every employee is a key employee, and it makes sense to provide these people with an equity stake in the company. A study completed in spring 2001 by Dr. Joseph Blasi of Rutgers University demonstrated that this theory—making more employees feel and act like owners through stock options compensation programs—makes good business sense. What Dr. Blasi and his colleagues discovered is that there is a distinct and positive correlation between companies that reward their employees with stock options and an increase in a company's overall productivity and profitability.

Stock options became a wildly popular compensation tool in the high-tech sector because they allowed cash-poor start-ups to preserve money for capital investments other than high salaries.

Stock options are another form of compensation. Just as your salary and other benefits (401k, medical and dental insurance, group life and/or disability insurance) allow you to support your current lifestyle, these tools allow you to plan for your future.

With proper use of stock option compensation, you can do the following:

1. Save money for the down payment on a new home or a new car.
2. Fund an education: yours, your children's, or your grandchildren's.
3. Provide for that long-awaited vacation or, even better, sabbatical.
4. Secure a comfortable and lengthy retirement.
5. Create a legacy for future generations.

Stock options can be a powerful tool for wealth accumulation, financial independence, and financial flexibility. Historically, stocks have provided a higher return on investment than have bonds or cash, and small company stocks have returned more than have large company stocks. That's not to say there haven't been periods of time—1929, 1973–1974, 1987, 1994, 2000–2002—when returns have been negative or experienced wild swings in valuation, but the overall trend has historically been positive and indicates that those willing to ride the roller coaster will enjoy long-term appreciation in the value of their equity assets.

Obviously, past performance is no guarantee of future performance and no one seems to have the perfect crystal ball, but history has taught us that the equity markets rise over time. This is the optimistic opinion of every stock option recipient from the mailroom to the boardroom.

You have been given stock options because your company believes you affect the financial performance it reports to shareholders both in the short term and in the long term.

The management of your company believes that an "ownership culture," a place where everyone thinks and acts like an owner, is a winning culture.

The managers have earmarked a certain amount of equity in the company for the employees because they understand that the greatest assets they have in today's competitive marketplace are not financial but human. *You* are the competitive advantage.

Management recognizes your contribution to the bottom line and wants to reward you for the commitment and sacrifice required for creating shareholder value.

Stock options almost always come with a vesting schedule. These are the "golden handcuffs" that keep employees around. And let's face it, it's a littler easier to work smarter, faster, and cheaper and stay with a company longer if you believe you will benefit financially.

The most common questions regarding stock options are:

"When should I exercise my stock options?" and "When should I sell the stock I have from exercising my options?"

The absolute answer to those questions is that it depends!

It depends on each individual's financial situation, resources, and goals. It's like asking: "Am I in love?" "When should we start a family?" or "Should I take that new job and move across the country?" It depends.

Strategic planning and management of your stock option compensation can mean a

20 to 40 percent increase

in your realized benefit of stock option compensation.

Exercising your options and selling your stock are decisions that should be made within the context of your unique financial circumstances.

Why do people exercise and sell stock options? Again, a variety of factors influence the exercise of stock options.

It may be to pay off debts; it may be to diversify an investment portfolio; it may be to buy a bigger house.

Unfortunately, most people exercise their options because the options are about to expire, or they are leaving the company, or they are in urgent need of cash. Those typical exercise situations are almost always reactive and tactical versus proactive and strategic.

Questions You Should Be Asking about Your Employee Stock Options

Now that you understand that you have everything to gain and nothing to lose, it's time to begin asking some important questions:

1. How much money do these stock options really represent after I pay to exercise them *and* pay the taxes?
2. What do I want to do with that money?
3. What are my top three financial priorities?
4. What are the risks involved in having these options?
5. What can I do to minimize my risk and maximize my return?

Unfortunately, most employees who receive stock options don't take the time to consider the strategic role equity compensation can play in their overall financial situation because they don't understand the opportunity being presented to them.

Chances are, you've spent more time preparing for your next vacation or buying a new car than you have researching and understanding your stock option compensation.

But before you learn more about your stock options, you need to learn more about yourself: what kind of an investor you are; what your real risk tolerance is; what your financial goals, fears, and aspirations may be; what obstacles stand between your success or failure in achieving those goals; and what steps you've taken toward your own financial well-being.

Chapter 2 will begin to prepare you for the paradigm shift you must complete to maximize your equity compensation and lay the foundation for realizing your potential for wealth accumulation. Read on to learn more about the formal planning process so that you can lay a strong financial foundation to build upon.

Chapter Checklist

• Know what your exercise price is for each stock option you've earned.

- Know the expiration date for each stock option you've earned.
- Begin to think about your strike price in the context of your company's historical stock market performance so that you can assess its viability as an investment, as well as compensation, and arrive at a logical target for selling your stock.

2

A LOOK IN THE MIRROR

This chapter introduces you to the formal financial planning process and provides a context within which to develop strategies and tactics related to stock option compensation. It is important to have a planning framework in mind as you progress through each chapter and learn more about equity compensation.

It's hard to think about tough questions when things are good. When you're young, retirement seems a lifetime away; when you're healthy, there's no reason to contemplate disability or death. But then it happens—those moments that matter.

As we witnessed the unthinkable horror of September 11, 2001, and let the magnitude of loss take root in our collective psyche, we were reminded of our inevitable mortality, the fragility of our everyday existence. We could no longer ignore the fact that the next plane ride could be our last, that we might not come home one day from the office, that random acts of violence can touch our lives just as easily as they can touch the lives of the people we see on the evening news.

Story after heart-wrenching story unfolded, telling of young families left to redefine their future with little or no resources or widows overwhelmed with the daunting task of inventorying a lifetime and divvying it up because no will or trust had been drawn

9

up. And every soul touched by the loss of a loved one, when asked if there was enough life insurance to give him or her some relief from the surreal circus that had become their new reality, would simply shake his or her head no and stare off into the land of unanswered questions.

The fact is, we don't like to look into the mirror and ask the "what if" questions; we don't even know all the questions we should ask. Defending ourselves from the bogeyman we've never seen, preparing for an event we've never encountered—not only is it abstract, it can seem downright absurd.

But for grown-ups in the real world, it's necessary. And those stock options you've been awarded are a very grown-up form of compensation that has put an exclamation point at the end of the phrase "it's necessary." It's time to figure out what you want, what you need, and how you're going to get there. No more "I've been meaning to get to that" or "One of these days I'll get around to it." Not because some unimagined disaster is about to descend upon you or death or disability might be lurking in the shadows; the fact is, stock option compensation can lead to some unexpected and expensive consequences that require more thought and planning than almost any other form of compensation available to today's workforce. You simply cannot afford to treat your finances casually any longer.

Like so many important things in life, just beginning the financial planning process is half the battle. So why do we procrastinate?

Some people feel invincible until something unfortunate happens.

Some people are embarrassed to admit they don't know everything and don't have everything done, and so they do nothing and save total embarrassment—and anger and frustration—for the family members left with the job of untangling their affairs.

For some folks, the more they learn about what there is to managing all the financial aspects of life, the more overwhelmed they become. This is the classic paralysis of analysis.

Then there are those who let the fear of doing something wrong or trusting someone with something so important cause them to pull back and insist on doing everything themselves, governed by

the inevitable limitations of a single mind's capacity for knowledge, creativity, and problem solving.

Many people have simply outgrown the people they've been working with, and they later learn the hard way that things change and we either change with them or pay the consequences.

But all those excuses, all those seemingly valid rationalizations for putting off formal planning, seem trivial when one is confronted with those moments that matter. Suddenly, you find yourself asking, "Why didn't I take the time to get that done?" or "What could have been more important than making sure my family was taken care of?"

Tackling the complexities of your stock option compensation—and it is convoluted—is a piece of a much bigger puzzle. It's an important piece, but it needs to be put in the proper context. Therefore, let's begin with the big picture and create a framework, a context for your equity compensation and the role it can play in an overall financial plan.

Formal financial planning is a process of clarifying your goals and objectives, identifying your resources and liabilities, and creating a road map for getting you from where you are today to where you want to be in the future. Effective planning also identifies the predictable obstacles you can or will encounter and helps you develop a strategy for overcoming those roadblocks.

Figure 2.1 is a *planning pyramid* that outlines a hierarchy of priorities that should be addressed in any financial planning process.

It's not uncommon to ignore a few of the building blocks at the base of the pyramid and skip to the areas we perceive to be more interesting, more exciting, or more fun. Unfortunately, that leaves us vulnerable in ways that become painfully obvious in our time, or more likely our family's time, of greatest need—when it's time to pay that tuition bill, when it's time to retire, when it's time to take care of that elderly parent who is no longer physically or financially independent. Good financial planning builds a rock-solid foundation on which to assemble your future and that of your family.

Fortune magazine's 1999 "Retirement Guide" reported those individuals with a formal financial plan acquire nearly five times the assets of those who don't go through the planning process. Compre-

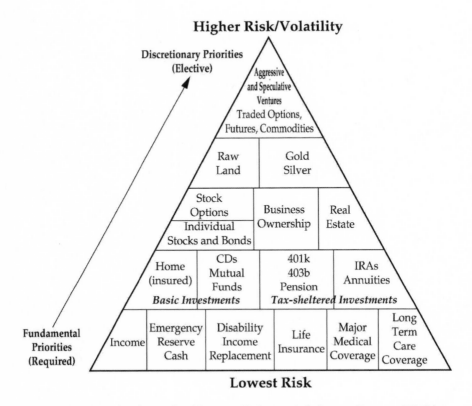

Figure 2.1 Survival needs. (*Source*: Private Advisory Group, LLC.)

hensive financial planning works because people who are committed
to planning become better stewards of their finances; they get what
they inspect, not what they expect. They employ professionals in
the evaluation and selection of products and services appropriate
for their circumstances. And they have the financial tools at their
disposal to monitor their financial life as well as they do their business affairs.

The financial planning process is analogous to creating a travel
itinerary: You begin by deciding where you want to go, how much
time you have to complete your journey, and what resources are
available to get the job done. With those details in mind, you can

begin to make decisions and determine any concessions you're willing to make to reach your ultimate goal.

The obstacle most people face in handling their own financial concerns is that they have competing priorities and become overwhelmed by the challenge of reconciling those priorities with limited resources. How do you fund life insurance, reduce your credit card debt, save for your child's college education, and maximize your contributions to your retirement savings plan with the same dollar? And where and when do stock options play a role in the whole process?

Too many people slip into a state of denial and procrastinate, avoiding these conflicting issues until a decision is forced upon them by external circumstances (the tuition check is due, your stock option award is about to expire, or you work another five years because you haven't set aside enough money for retirement). These represent reactions, not strategies.

If you can find the time to take your car in for an oil change every so often, don't you think you should make the time to "fine-tune" your overall financial well-being?

A proactive approach—one that will allow you to maximize the potential of your stock option compensation as it relates to your unique circumstances—is to begin a formal planning process. Here's the magic formula:

Inspection + Introspection = Baseline

Inspection: what you have, what you owe, and what you want (numerically driven)

Introspection: who you are, what you value, what you fear, your definition of success, and your definition of independence (emotionally driven)

Baseline: the starting point from which all progress is measured

Any effective planning process embraces the fact that human beings make decisions on the basis of emotions, not logic, and begins with an in-depth series of questions designed to bring structure to what may otherwise seem esoteric: the introspection part of the formula. Providing a framework for the numerical aspects of your plan and then creating a method for measuring your progress are actually much easier.

As an example, a simple spreadsheet that measures the difference between the price you paid for a stock and the price for which you sold it provides a straightforward mathematical calculation that allows you to determine whether you made money or lost money on that particular investment.

The spreadsheet will not, however, indicate how you decided to purchase that stock in the first place and/or what led you to sell it at the time you did. And your buy-sell criteria—which in this scenario you have no way of measuring—ultimately determines your long-term investment success.

It isn't the results associated with the purchase or sale of a single stock, mutual fund, or piece of property that will determine your eventual success; it's the decision-making process you employ and your ability to adhere to it over time that will ultimately determine the outcome.

So where should you begin? How do you develop your own road map for success and put your stock option compensation in the proper context? How do you provide yourself with the necessary structure for making decisions aligned with your unique circumstances and drown out the clutter of the media hype and office chatter?

The following are some questions that should be asked at the outset of the formal planning process. A more comprehensive list would be used in an actual discovery interview, but these questions are particularly useful in acquainting you with the thought process you need to begin:

- What is the most important thing that money gives you today?
- What would you do differently if you had the money?
- What are your three most important financial goals?
- What concerns you most about your financial future?

- At what age do you want to be financially independent, meaning that you could "retire" from the job you have now to pursue other passions?
- Would you wish your family to maintain your current standard of living in the event of your death?
- What do you want to have happen to your estate when you die? What arrangements have you made to ensure that those wishes will be fulfilled?
- If you became disabled and couldn't work, where would your income come from? How long could it support your family's current standard of living?
- Are there any significant financial changes or decisions you will be facing in the next few years?
- What would you consider a good investment?
- What characteristics do you evaluate when considering where to invest your money?
- If you had to describe your investment temperament or style, what would it be?
- What does the term *asset allocation* mean to you?
- What was your pretax total portfolio return for last year?
- What percent of your investment assets is concentrated in your company's stock?
- What is the true value of your stock option compensation if you cashed out today (after paying taxes, brokerage fees, etc.)?
- What role does your stock option compensation play in your overall investment strategy? Why?
- How do you decide when to exercise your stock options?
- What determines when you sell the stock you've acquired after exercising those options?
- What is the historical trading range for your company's stock?
- What price targets have you set for exercising your options? Why?

These are questions we don't often ask ourselves and almost never answer. These are also questions we don't always discuss with our spouses or loved ones unless a neutral third party is sitting across the table, patiently demanding that we verbalize our thoughts and feelings regarding such matters.

Stock option compensation simply adds emphasis to the need for completing this process. Effective financial planning has a lot of "moving parts"; stock option compensation adds a level of complexity that makes it even more important. You've earned your stock options. Don't let procrastination and ignorance rob you and your family of an important wealth-building tool that not only should be realized but ideally should be optimized.

But answering these types of questions is only half the battle. Answering them and then using the answers to create a meaningful context for putting the information into an organized, measurable framework that allows you to create a road map, monitor your progress, and revise your game plan as circumstances change is the true power of comprehensive planning.

What kinds of tools and measuring sticks can you expect from this process? A formal plan should include but is not limited to the following:

- Cash Flow Analysis (showing you where the money comes from and where it ultimately goes). Figures 2.2 and 2.3 illustrate this analysis.
- Net Worth Statement (an inventory of your assets and liabilities). Figures 2.4 and 2.5 represent a typical summary report.
- Option Optimization Analysis (illustrating multiple exercise strategies that anticipate tax consequences, historical stock price performance, insider buying/selling activity, personal financial objectives and timelines, etc.,...all the variables that will be uncovered in the Optioneering® process discussed later in the book).
- Disability Income/Long-term Care Needs Analysis (illustrating your income replacement needs over a variety of time periods—three months, six months, one year, five years, lifetime—in the event that you cannot work and fund your financial objectives or require long-term care during your retirement years). Figure 2.6 graphically represents this concept.
- Survivor Needs Analysis (illustrating your life insurance needs as they relate to providing for your family's needs if you die prematurely). Figure 2.7 demonstrates the needs in this area.

- Accumulation Goal Projections (outlining the funding require-ments you should target on a monthly or annual basis to achieve your stated financial objectives: education funding, retirement funding, starting a new business, etc.). Figures 2.8 through 2.13 are examples of the analysis you might review.
- Asset Allocation Model (a recommended investment allocation strategy aligned with your risk tolerance, resources, rate of return assumptions, and time frame for investing). Figures 2.14 and 2.15 provide you with illustrations of this concept.
- Investment Policy Statement (a document that provides the guidelines for your long-term investment decisions). A sample of this tool is included in the appendixes.
- Estate Plan Analysis (a review of wills, trusts, contracts, and bene-ficiary designations to determine the consequences of your death, both today and at life expectancy, for your estate and your inten-ded heirs). Figure 2.16 is a simple but powerful graphic depicting the consequences of estate taxes.
- The Impact of Inflation, Taxes, and Real Rates of Return (demon-strates the influence these have on your ability to create and keep wealth). Figure 2.17 provides an illustration of these key concepts.

Once you've created this basic framework and have an organized context within which to view your situation, you are free to play out multiple "what if" scenarios:

- What if you wanted to retire three years earlier than planned?
- What if your son wanted to go to a private university instead of a state school?
- What if you wanted to take a few years off to "recharge your bat-teries" or take a less stressful job at a lower salary?
- What if you used the proceeds of your stock options to pay off the mortgage as opposed to investing the cash in stock market assets?
- What if you only made 7 percent in your 401k account instead of 9 percent?
- What if you exercised all your vested options this year because you wanted to quit and take a job with another company?

- What impact will executing a disqualifying disposition on your incentive stock options have in terms of current-year taxes and your contribution to your retirement savings goal?

The list goes on and on.

Amazingly, most people operate without the benefit of comprehensive financial planning. As the old adage goes, "People don't plan to fail, they fail to plan." Stock option compensation should be the catalyst that pushes you into the formal planning process and helps you develop a personal blueprint for success.

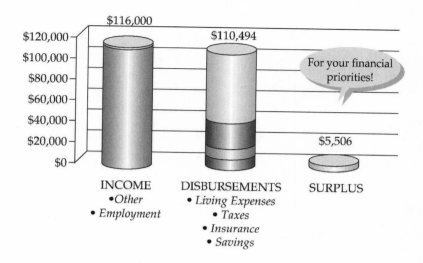

	Annual Amount	Percentage of Total Income
Income		
Employment	$114,000	98%
Other	2,000	2%
Total	$116,000	100%
Disbursements		
Living Expenses	$66,140	57%
Taxes	24,444	21%
Insurance	10,010	9%
Savings/Retirement Plans	9,900	9%
Total	110,494	95%
Surplus	**$5,506**	**5%**
Additional Savings Goal	**$2,400**	**2%**

Figure 2.2 Cash flow summary.

	Annual Amount	Monthly Average	Percent of Total Income
Income			
Employment - Tom			
Employment - Marilyn	$60,000	$5,000	52%
Interest and Dividends - Tom	54,000	4,500	47%
Interest and Dividends - Marilyn	1,400	117	1%
	600	50	1%
Total Income	$116,000	$9,667	100%
Disbursements			
Expenses			
Housing			
Child Care	$24,000	$2,000	21%
Transportation	600	50	1%
Food and Beverages	7,800	650	7%
Clothing	5,400	450	5%
Furnishings	2,400	200	2%
Personal Care and Cash	1,500	125	1%
Medical/Dental/Drugs	4,800	400	4%
Education/Self-Improvement	1,440	120	1%
Debt/Installment Payments	3,000	250	3%
Entertainment	3,600	300	3%
Vacations and Holidays	4,200	350	4%
Charitable Contributions	4,800	400	4%
Reinvested Interest	1,200	100	1%
Pet Care	1,200	100	1%
	200	17	0%
Total Expenses	$66,140	$5,512	57%
Taxes			
Federal - Tom	$8,400	$700	7%
Federal - Marilyn	6,000	500	5%
State - Tom	2,400	200	2%
State - Marilyn	2,040	170	2%
OASDI/Medicare	5,604	467	5%
Total Taxes	$24,444	$2,037	21%
Insurance			
Allstar VUL	$3,600	$300	3%
Allstar Level Term	900	75	1%
American Life Group Term	350	29	0%
Metro Group Insurance	250	21	0%
Employer LTD	150	13	0%
All American Disability	1,100	92	1%
Umbrella Liability	180	15	0%

Figure 2.3 Cash flow.

Homeowners	600	50	1%
Medical	1,280	107	1%
Auto	1,600	133	1%
Total Insurance	$10,010	$834	9%

Savings

AIM Charter Fund B	$1,500	$125	1%
Atlas Retirement Plan	2,400	200	2%
Saamco Growth and Income	900	75	1%
Putnam Voyager II M	900	75	1%
Medical Center 403(b)	3,000	250	3%
Voyager Index Fund	1,200	100	1%
Total Savings	$9,900	$825	9%

Total Disbursements	$110,494	$9,208	95%

Surplus	**$5,506**	**$459**	**5%**
Additional Savings Goal	**$2,400**	**$200**	**2%**

Figure 2.3 (cont.) Cash flow.

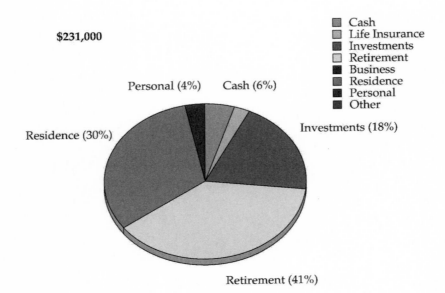

Asset	Market Value	Liability	Net Worth	Percent of Net Worth
Cash and Checking	$15,000	$0	$15,000	6%
Life Insurance Cash Values	8,000	0	8,000	3%
Investments:				
Bonds & Stocks	37,000	0	37,000	16%
Speculative & Collectibles	4,000	0	4,000	2%
Retirement Plans	95,000	0	95,000	41%
Residence(s)	180,000	(110,000)	70,000	30%
Personal Property	25,000	(15,000)	10,000	4%
Other	0	(8,000)	(8,000)	(3%)
Totals	$364,000	($133,000)	$231,000	100%

Figure 2.4 Net worth summary by asset type.

Asset	Owner	Assumed Rate of Return	Market Value	Liability	Net Worth
Cash and Checking					
Bank of Irvine Checking	Community	1.50%	$4,000	$0	$4,000
Savings, CD's, T-Bills					
Putnam Money Market	Community	5.00%	6,000	0	6,000
Bank of Irvine CD	Community	4.00%	5,000	0	5,000
Tax Free Bond Funds					
CA-Muni Tax Free Bond Fund	Tom	8.00%	10,000	0	10,000
Stocks/Growth Funds					
AIM Charter Fund B	Community	10.00%	5,000	0	5,000
Saamco Growth and Income	Community	9.00%	10,000	0	10,000
Putnam Voyager II M	Community	10.00%	4,000	0	4,000
Voyager Index Fund	Community	10.50%	8,000	0	8,000
Residence					
123 Main Street	Community	3.00%	180,000	(110,000)	70,000
Personal Property					
Vehicles	Community	0.00%	25,000	(15,000)	10,000
Collectibles					
Coin Collection	Marilyn	0.00%	4,000	0	4,000
Other Liabilities					
Citibank VISA Credit Card	Community	0.00%	0	(8,000)	(8,000)
401(k)					
Atlas Retirement Plan	Tom	10.00%	30,000	0	30,000
TSA/403(b)					
Medical Center 403(b)	Marilyn	11.00%	65,000	0	65,000
Life Insurance Cash Values					
Allstar VUL	Tom	--	8,000	--	8,000
Total			**$364,000**	**($133,000)**	**$231,000**

Figure 2.5 Net worth statement.

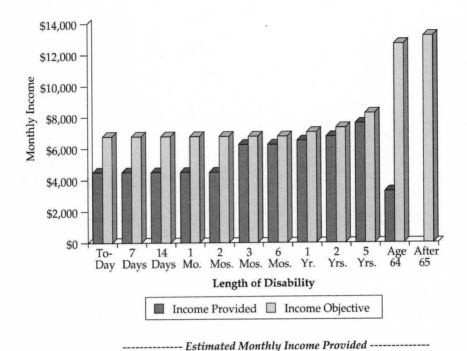

| | ------------- Estimated Monthly Income Provided ------------- | | | | |
Need	Monthly Income Objective[1]	Marilyn's Earnings[2]	Social Security and Group Insurance	Personal Disability Insurance	Other	Income Surplus/ (Shortage)
Today	$6,767	$4,500	$0	$0	$0	($2,267)
After 7 Days	6,767	4,500	0	0	0	(2,267)
After 14 Days	6,767	4,500	0	0	0	(2,267)
After 1 Month	6,767	4,500	0	0	0	(2,267)
After 2 Months	6,767	4,500	0	0	0	(2,267)
After 3 Months	6,767	4,500	1,750	0	0	(517)
After 6 Months	6,767	4,500	1,750	0	0	(517)
After 1 Year	7,037	4,680	1,820	0	0	(537)
After 2 Years	7,319	4,867	1,893	0	0	(559)
After 5 Years	8,233	5,475	2,129	0	0	(629)
Age 64	12,674	0	3,278	0	0	(9,396)
After 65	13,181	0	0	0	0	(13,181)

[1]Increases at the assumed rate of inflation of 4.00%.
[2]Increases annually by 4.00%.

Figure 2.6 Disability income needs.

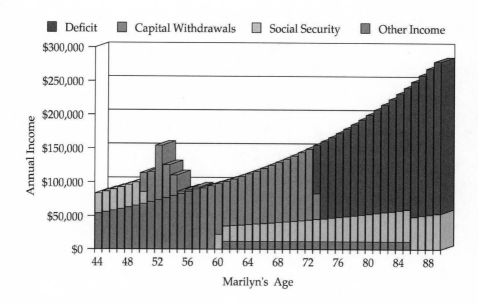

Income needs:

At Marilyn's age:	44	51	58
Annual income desired	$78,000	$111,338	$91,172
Income available:	83,426	71,060	0
Annual surplus/(shortage)	**$5,426**	**($40,278)**	**($91,172)**
Assets available at Tom's death			$147,000
Life insurance death benefits			350,000
Total capital available			$497,000
Immediate Cash needs			(193,340)
Net capital available for income needs			**$303,660**

Additional capital needed today to fund all income shortages and provide for your
survivor's needs until Marilyn's age 90 is $138,170.[1]

These results are hypothetical and are not a promise of future performance.
[1]Calculated based on an assumed rate of return of 5.00%.

Figure 2.7 Survivor needs. Capital analysis.

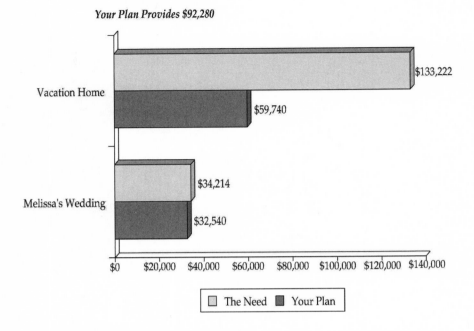

Total Need $167,436

Your Plan Provides $92,280

This graph illustrates the projected capital needed to achieve your accumulation objective(s) and how your projected current savings and investments are helping meet this goal.

		Funding Alternatives[1]		
	Amount Needed Per Year (Today's $)	*Additional Sum[1]*	*Additional Monthly Level Savings*	*Additional Monthly Inflating Savings[2]*
Goal				
Vacation Home	$90,000	$37,354	$427	$364
Melissa's Wedding	25,000	975	13	12
Totals	**$115,000**	**$38,329**	**$440**	**$375**

[1]Single-sum investment alternative assumes that existing savings will continue and Funding Alternatives earn a rate of return of 7.00%.

[2]The amount shown is for the first year only; this amount must be increased annually by the assumed inflation rate of 4.00%.

These results are hypothetical and are not a promise of future performance.

Figure 2.8 Accumulation goals.

How will you meet the rising cost of education?

School	Annual 2001-2002	Total 4 Years Cost in 2010 *
University of Arizona	$9,020	$62,892
Duke University	$34,368	$239,630
Havard University	$32,507	$226,654
University of Nebraska	$8,218	$57,300
Michigan State	$10,403	$72,535
Stanford	$35,301	$246,135
Yale University	$34,749	$242,286
UC-Irvine	$11,217	$78,210

	Average Annual Increases		
	Public College[2]	Private College[2]	Consumer Price Index[3]
1992	6.5%	7.2%	2.9%
1993	5.9%	5.1%	2.7%
1994	5.0%	5.6%	2.7%
1995	4.7%	4.8%	2.5%
1996	4.3%	5.4%	3.3%
1997	5.0%	5.1%	1.7%
1998	3.9%	4.0%	1.6%
1999	4.1%	4.9%	2.7%
2000	3.0%	5.0%	3.4%
2001	6.3%	5.6%	1.6%

Source: *Assumes college costs increase at 6% annually.
[1]ASC 2001-2002 Standard Research Compilation Undergraduate Institutions. Copyright © 2001, College Entrance Examination Board. All Rights Reserved.
[2]Source: The College Board, Trends in College Pricing. Copyright © 2001 by College Entrance Examination Board. All rights reserved. College costs include tuition and fees and room and board. Based on academic year.
[3]Source: Bureau of Labor Statistics, Consumer Price Index All Urban Consumers (CPI-U) Based on calendar year.

Figure 2.9 Cost of education.

Education Needs:

Goal Number	Name	School	Annual Amount Needed	Years Until Needed	Years Needed	Inflated at	Amount Needed Future Dollars
1	Melissa	Univ. of California: Irvine	$11,217	6	4	6.00%	$69,607
2	Neal	Univ. of Nevada: Las Vegas	14,836	7	4	6.00%	97,588

Total amount needed - future dollars   **$167,195**

Assets and Savings Available:

Name	Current Market Value	Monthly Savings Amount	Year Savings Start	Number of Years to Save	Assigned to Goal
Saamco Growth and Income	$10,000	$75	2000	9	1
Putnam Voyager II M	4,000	75	2000	10	2
Grandparents CD for Melissa	12,000	0	2000	9	1
Grandparents CD for Neal	12,000	0	2000	10	2
Total	**$38,000**				

Funding Alternatives:

	Amount Needed Future Dollars	Existing Plan Provides	Additional Amount Needed[1] Single Sum	Monthly Level Savings	Monthly Inflating Savings[2]
Melissa	$69,607	$46,059	$13,534	$162	$140
Neal	97,588	38,329	33,528	369	314
Total	**$167,195**	**$84,388**	**$47,062**	**$531**	**$454**

[1]All additional savings begin today and assume a rate of return of 6.00%.
[2]Inflating savings will increase annually by 4.00%.

Figure 2.10 Education goals. Summary.

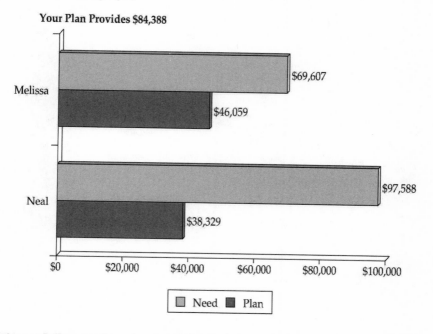

Total Need $167,195

Your Plan Provides $84,388

This graph illustrates the projected capital needed to meet your education objectives and how your projected current savings and investments are helping meet the objectives.

Name	Amount Needed Per Year (Today's $)	Sum[1]	Funding Alternatives[1]	
			Additional Monthly Level Savings	Additional Monthly Inflating Savings[2]
Melissa	$11,217	$13,534	$162	$140
Neal	14,836	33,528	369	314
		Additional		
Totals	$26,053	$47,062	$531	$454

[1]Single-sum investment alternative assumes that existing savings will continue and Funding Alternatives earn a rate of return of 6.00%.

[2]The amount shown is for the first year only; this amount must be increased annually by the assumed inflation rate of 4.00%.

These results are hypothetical and are not a promise of future performance.

Figure 2.11 Education funding goals.

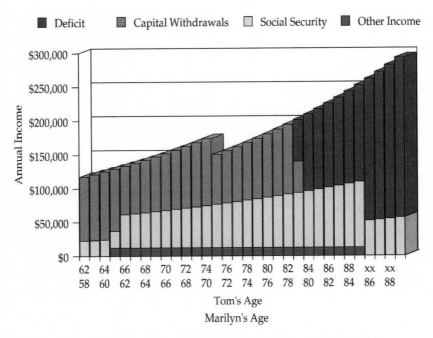

Assuming: Tom's mortality age 90, Marilyn's mortality age 90

Based on the current assets and income sources available during period shown, your financial objectives will be satisfied until Tom's age 83.

At Tom's Age	At Marilyn's Age	Annual Income Desired —Present Value	Annual Income Desired —Future Value	Direct Income Sources	Capital Withdrawal	Remaining Balance/ (Deficit)
62	58	$78,000	$117,511	$22,661	$94,849	$200,334
75	71	60,000	150,402	76,554	73,847	460,269

To provide your desired income you will need additional capital, at Tom's age 62, of $110,443.[1]

[1]Calculated based on an assumed rate of return of 8.00%.
These results are hypothetical and are not a promise of future performance.

Figure 2.12 Financial independence. Capital analysis.

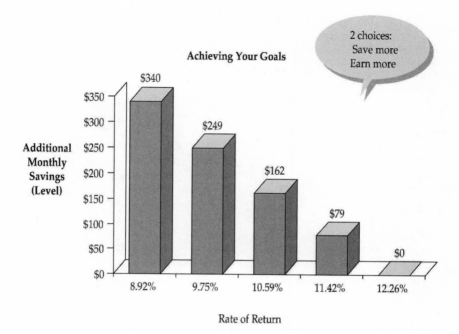

To reach your retirement goals based on the assumptions defined earlier, it is estimated that you need to accumulate $110,443 in 14 years.

The graph above shows how different rates of return affect the amount of money you must save monthly in order to achieve your retirement capital goal.

To accrue this additional capital when Tom is age 62, there are several options:

(a) **Save More** - Increase the amount of money you save each month at your current portfolio assumed rate of return. The 8.92% rate in the above graph represents your current effective portfolio assumed rate of return of your existing assets and savings, excluding deferred retirement plans, from now until age 62. If this rate is used for any additional savings, an additional monthly amount of $340 is required to achieve your goals.

(b) **Earn More** - Consider increasing your effective assumed rate of return by adjusting your asset allocation.

(c) **Save More/Earn More** - Combine option (a) "save more" and option (b) "earn more."

These results are hypothetical and are not a promise of future performance.

Figure 2.13 Save more—earn more.

Asset allocation is the process of combining asset classes such as stocks, bonds, and cash in a portfolio in order to meet your goals.

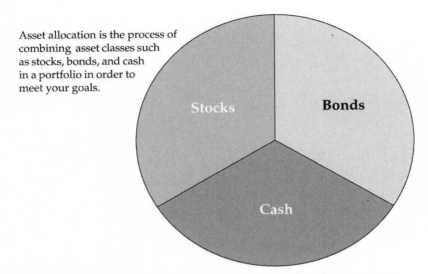

This is for illustrative purposes only and not indicative of any investment. Past performance is no guarantee of future results. Copyright 2002 Ibbotson Associates, Inc.

The asset allocation decision is one of the most important factors in determining both the return and the risk of an investment portfolio.

Asset allocation is the process of developing a diversified investment portfolio by combining different assets in varying proportions.

An asset is anything that produces income or can be purchased and sold, such as stocks, bonds, or certificates of deposit (CDs). Asset classes are groupings of assets with similar characteristics and properties. Examples of asset classes are large company stocks, long-term government bonds, and Treasury bills.

Every asset class has distinct characteristics and may perform differently in response to market changes. Therefore, careful consideration must be given to determine which assets you should hold and the amount you should allocate to each asset.

Factors that greatly influence the asset allocation decision are your financial needs and goals, the length of your investment horizon, and your attitude towards risk.

Diversification does not guarantee against loss. It is a method used to help manage investment risk.

Figure 2.14 What is asset allocation?

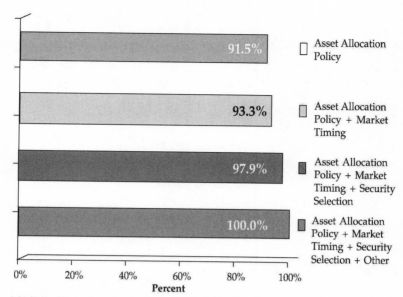

Asset Allocation Policy — 91.5%

Asset Allocation Policy + Market Timing — 93.3%

Asset Allocation Policy + Market Timing + Security Selection — 97.9%

Asset Allocation Policy + Market Timing + Security Selection + Other — 100.0%

This is for illustrative purposes only and not indicative of any investment.
Past performance is no guarantee of future results. Copyright 2001 Ibbotson Associates, Inc.

A portfolio's long-term performance is determined primarily by the distribution of dollars among asset classes, such as stocks, bonds, and cash equivalents.

The asset allocation decision is one of the most important decisions you will make as an investor. You may think that security selection and market timing are the primary components driving a portfolio's performance, but these factors are only important when combined with a strategic asset allocation policy.

Recent studies found that a portfolio's asset allocation policy dominates portfolio performance and, over a period of time, typically explains over 90% of the variation in the portfolio's returns. This far exceeds the effects of both market timing and security selection, demonstrating that the asset allocation decision is the most important determinant of portfolio performance.

Note: The study, "Determinants of Portfolio Performance," by Gary P. Brinson, L. Randolph Hood, and Gilbert L. Beebower, was published in the July/August 1986 edition of the Financial Analysts Journal. *This study was updated by Brinson, Brian D. Singer, and Beebower in the May/June 1991 edition of the* Financial Analysts Journal. *The update analyzed quarterly data from 82 large U.S. pension plans over the period 1977-1987. Past performance is no guarantee of future results.*
Source: Brinson, Gary P. et al. "Determinants of Portfolio Performance," *Financial Analysts Journal*, July/August 1986. Updated in *Financial Analysts Journal*, May/June 1991.

Figure 2.15 Importance of strategic asset allocation. Contributing factors of portfolio performance.

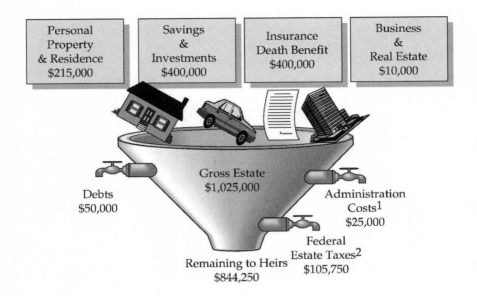

This illustration demonstrates what might happen to your estate if no planning has been done. It does not include any insurance proceeds from an irrevocable trust or from a policy owned by another person. At death, debts, estate taxes and administrative fees must be paid from the estate value.

What will be left for your heirs?

[1]Administrative costs are assumed to be 4.00% of your current, gross estate.
[2]Taxes are based on the 2002 Federal Estate Tax Tables.

Figure 2.16 Estate cost estimator.

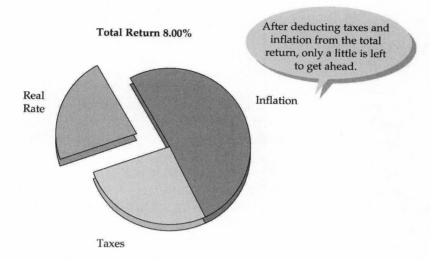

Total Return 8.00%

After deducting taxes and inflation from the total return, only a little is left to get ahead.

Real Rate

Inflation

Taxes

Your real rate of return is 1.77%.

The real rate of return is calculated as follows:

Gross Rate of Return	8.00%
Less Taxes (8.00% times 27.00%)	(2.16%)
After Tax Rate of Return	5.84%

During the year, however, inflation has had an impact on your purchasing power. Therefore, in order to calculate the Real Rate of Return, inflation must be accounted for as follows:

$$(\frac{1 + \text{After Tax Rate of Return}}{1+ \text{Inflation}} - 1) \text{ times } 100 = \text{Real Rate of Return}$$

OR

$$(\frac{1 + 0.0584}{1 + 0.0400} - 1) \text{ times } 100 = 1.77\%$$

This is a hypothetical illustration only and is not indicative of the performance of any particular investment. Assumes 27.00% marginal tax rate and 4.00% inflation.

Figure 2.17 Real rate of return.

Chapter Checklist

- Schedule a time to begin your formal financial planning process.
- Recognize the need to work with qualified professionals.
- Commit to an annual financial "check up."
- Begin to identify the resources and tools you will use to stay on course.
- Measure your results on a consistent basis.
- Plan, review, and revise based on your objectives.
- Remain flexible and understand that your goals will change over time.

3

Types of Employee Stock Options

This chapter outlines the differences between the four most common types of stock options and helps you understand the key characteristics that distinguish one type from another.

Nonqualified Stock Options

Nonqualified stock options represent a cash equivalent opportunity to buy company stock. Think about these options as a complicated cash bonus award.

Nonqualified stock options (NQSOs) are employee stock options that do not satisfy the requirements of a statutory stock option under the Internal Revenue System (IRS) Code; Section 422.

In plain English, they are not eligible for favorable tax treatment and are considered compensation to the employee *when they are exercised.* There are no tax consequences when the stock options are granted, only when the option is exercised—when the recipient actually takes ownership of the stock.

Nonqualified stock options are generally nontransferable, although there are many exceptions to that rule [in the wake of the 1996 Securities and Exchange Commission (SEC) amendments, more and more companies are amending their plans to allow for limited transferability, and so reviewing the plan document is critical]. They are almost always subject to a vesting schedule and can be used to compensate nonemployees (independent contractors, nonemployee board members, outside consultants, etc.)

At the time of exercise, the recipient is taxed on the difference between the grant price and the fair market value of the company's stock on the day of exercise. That "spread" is subject to Social Security, Medicare, and ordinary income taxes regardless of whether the shares are sold or held for investment—hence the characterization as a cash equivalent form of compensation. Figures 3.1 through 3.5 demonstrate the tax consequences of exercising NQSOs.

From the IRS's perspective, the value the recipient realizes on the date of exercise is classified as if it were a cash bonus. Such tax treatment leads many NQSO holders to execute a "cashless exercise" that results in a simultaneous exercise of options and immediate sale of company stock, in essence allowing the recipient to realize the cash benefit and meet the corresponding tax liabilities without taking more risk related to the fluctuation of the stock's market price.

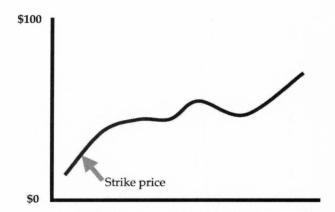

Figure 3.1 NQSOs. Tax consequences. (© Net Worth Strategies, Inc. 2002)

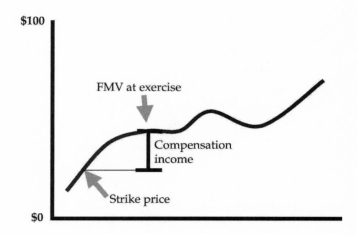

Figure 3.2 NQSOs. (© Net Worth Strategies, Inc. 2002)

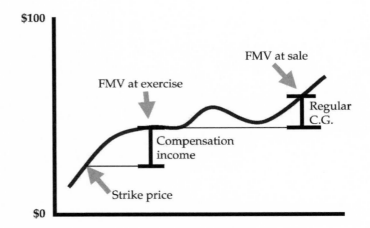

Figure 3.3 NQSOs. (© Net Worth Strategies, Inc. 2002)

- Example
  - Joe Client has 5,000 NQSOs
  - Strike price is $10, FMV of Stock is $50
  - Regular tax and tentative minimum tax equal
  - Combined tax rate 45.82 percent (38.6 percent income,
    1.45 percent medicare, above Soc. Sec. limit, 5.77 percent CA net)
  - Tax Effects at exercise:

NQSOs Exercised	5,000
Bargain Element (50–10)	$ 40
Taxable compensation	$ 200,000
Combined tax rate	45.82 percent
Tax liability on exercise	$ 91,640

Figure 3.4 NQSOs. (© Net Worth Strategies, Inc. 2002)

- Example cont'd
  - Cash flow effects from exercise:

NQSOs Exercised		5,000
Strike Price	$	10
Cash to company	$	50,000
Total taxes due	$	91,640
Total cash outflow	$	141,640

  - Cash flow from immediate sale:

Number of shares sold		5,000
FMV of stock	$	50
Gross cash inflow	$	250,000
Less cash outflow	$	(141,640)
Net cash inflow	$	108,360

Figure 3.5 NQSOs. (© Net Worth Strategies, Inc. 2002)

Incentive Stock Options

This form of equity compensation, unlike NQSOs, is intended to be a company stock award (as opposed to a cash equivalent award). Think about this type of option as a potential stock ownership award.

Incentive stock options (ISOs) do meet the requirements of Section 422(b) of the IRS Code and therefore qualify for preferential tax treatment under Section 421 of the code.

In simple terms, that means that an ISO has no Social Security, Medicare, or ordinary income tax consequences at the time of grant or the time of exercise.

Instead, employees are subject to taxation at the time they sell the shares of stock bought upon exercising the option.

If the stock is exercised and then sold less than one year from the date of exercise or two years from the date it was granted, that disqualifies the stock from receiving favorable tax treatment and the ISO reverts back to an NQSO for tax purposes. Basically, the "spread" is then considered compensation and is subject to payroll and income taxes. Figures 3.6 through 3.12 illustrate the tax implications of a disqualifying disposition of ISOs, depending on whether the sale takes place in a specific calendar year or simply within a twelve-month period.

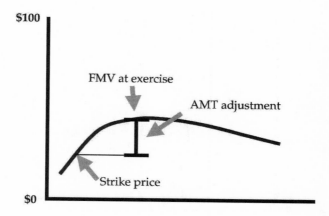

Figure 3.6 ISOs. Tax consequences, disqualifying disposition (same tax year). (© Net Worth Strategies, Inc. 2002)

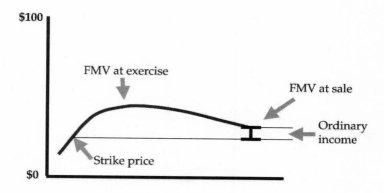

Figure 3.7 ISOs. Tax consequences, disqualifying disposition (same tax year). (© Net Worth Strategies, Inc. 2002)

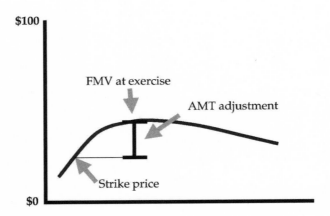

Figure 3.8 ISOs. Tax consequences, disqualifying disposition (*next* tax year). (© Net Worth Strategies, Inc. 2002)

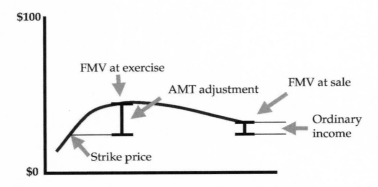

Figure 3.9 Tax consequences, disqualifying disposition (*next* tax year). (© Net Worth Strategies, Inc. 2002)

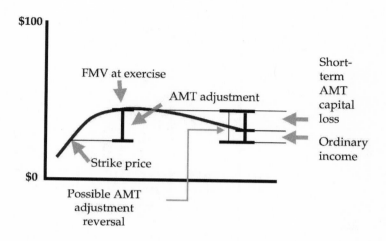

Figure 3.10 Tax consequences, disqualifying disposition (*next* tax year). (© Net Worth Strategies, Inc. 2002)

- Example

  - Tax effects from disqualifying sale in year of exercise at $20 FMV:

	Regular	AMT
Number of shares sold	5,000	5,000
FMV of stock	$ 20	$ 20
Gross cash inflow	$ 100,000	100,000
Cost basis	$ (50,000)	(50,000)
Ordinary income	$ 50,000	50,000
Reversal AMT adjustment		$ 0
Combined ordinary tax rate	45.82%	
Ordinary tax	$ 22,910	
Total net cash	27,090	

Figure 3.11 ISOs. (© Net Worth Strategies, Inc. 2002)

- Example
  - Tax effects from disqualifying sale in year after exercise at $20 FMV:

	Regular	AMT
Number of shares sold	5,000	5,000
FMV of stock	$ 20	$ 20
Gross cash inflow	$ 100,000	100,000
Cost basis	$ (50,000)	(250,000)
Ordinary Income	$ 50,000	
Short-term capital loss		$ (150,000)
Reversal AMT adjustment		$ 53,000
Combined ordinary tax rate	45.82%	
Ordinary tax	$ 22,910	
AMT tax credit	$ (22,910)	
Total net cash	$ (6,000)	

Figure 3.12 ISOs. (© Net Worth Strategies, Inc. 2002)

If, however, the employee exercises and holds the stock for one year and one day (and two years and one day from the date of grant), subsequent sales transactions will meet the requirements for favorable tax status and be taxed at long-term capital gains rates (20 percent). This is the most enticing aspect of ISOs and provides the incentive for employees to exercise them and take the risk associated with holding the shares and enduring the market fluctuation related to the share price as opposed to cashing out immediately, as is often the case with NQSOs. But...

An unexpected consequence of exercising incentive stock options is that the employee may be subjected to the alternative minimum tax (AMT). We will spend some time on this topic in another chapter, but be aware that there are strings attached to ISOs and that those strings cannot be ignored without some unintended and often expensive consequences. Figures 3.13 through 3.17 depict the result of a qualifying sale (disposition) of ISOs.

Incentive stock options can only be granted to employees and cannot be transferred (an employee cannot give or sell his or her options to someone else). No more than $100,000 of ISOs (valued at the grant price) can be deemed "exercisable" in any single year. ISOs that could be exercised and are in excess of $100,000 are converted to NQSOs, whether they are actually exercised or not, for tax purposes.

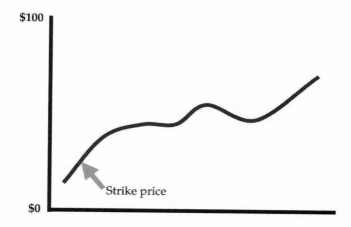

Figure 3.13 ISOs. (© Net Worth Strategies, Inc. 2002)

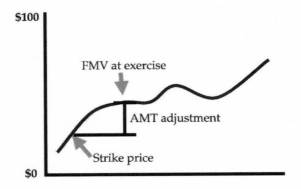

Figure 3.14 ISOs. (© Net Worth Strategies, Inc. 2002)

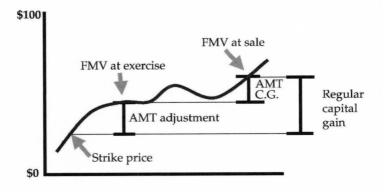

Figure 3.15 ISOs. (© Net Worth Strategies, Inc. 2002)

- Example
  - Same facts as NQSO example
  - Tax effects at exercise:

ISOs Exercised		5,000
Bargain Element (50-10)	$	40
Positive AMT adjustment	$	200,000
AMT tax rate		28%
Alternative minimum tax	$	56,000

  - Cash outflow at exercise:

ISOs exercised		5,000
Strike price	$	10
Cash to company	$	50,000
Total taxes due	$	56,000
Total cash outflow		106,000

Figure 3.16 ISOs. (© Net Worth Strategies, Inc. 2002)

- Example cont'd
  - Tax effects from sale after one year at $55 FMV:

	Regular	AMT
Number of shares sold	5,000	5,000
FMV of stock	$ 55	$ 55
Gross cash inflow	$ 275,000	275,000
Cost basis	$ (50,000)	(250,000)
Long-term capital gain	$ 225,000	25,000
Reversal AMT adjustment		$ 200,000
Capital gains tax rate	20%	
Capital gains tax	$ 45,000	
AMT tax credit	(45,000)	
Total net cash	169,000	

Figure 3.17 ISOs. (© Net Worth Strategies, Inc. 2002)

Employee Stock Purchase Plans

Intended as a way for employees to purchase shares of company stock—an investment program as opposed to a compensation plan—employee stock purchase plans (ESPPs) are one of the more popular tools used by companies to create an ownership culture. Think of this program as a way to invest in your company's stock cost-effectively.

The National Center for Employee Ownership estimates that 15.7 million employees in 4,000 companies currently purchase company stock through ESPP programs. Over 70 percent of the employees participating in these programs do so in a tax-qualified 423 plan (see Table 3.1 for qualifying requirements), meaning that employees can benefit from favorable tax treatment if they meet the holding requirements of one year and one day after the date of purchase and two years and one day after the beginning of the offering period. An ESPP qualifies under Section 423 of the IRS Code, but it is not an incentive stock option plan.

An ESPP works as a way for employees to buy company stock, often offered at a discount not exceeding 15 percent of the fair market value on the date of purchase, through payroll deductions. One of the most attractive aspects of many of these plans is their use of a "look-back" provision which allows the purchase price to be determined by using the value of the stock at the beginning of the offering period or on the purchase date, whichever is lower. Thus, an employee could profit from the purchase of company stock even in a declining market.

Like ISOs, qualified ESPP programs make it possible for employees to buy stock without tax consequences until the stock is sold.

Unlike the case with ISOs, employees are not subject to AMT when shares are purchased as part of a qualified ESPP, an employee can pay for company stock through payroll deductions, and no vesting period is associated with these plans.

If an employee receives a discount on the purchase of company stock under an ESPP program, he or she will have to report the *discount element* as compensation income at the time of selling the stock, but if the holding requirements are met or the employee dies while owning the shares, sale of the stock will qualify for long-term capital

Table 3.1. Employee Stock Purchase Plans, Section 423 Plan Requirements

- Available to employees only (not outside directors or consultants)
- The right to purchase shares in this program belongs only to the employee (meaning this is a nontransferable right to participate)
- All full-time employees must be eligible to participate
  - The company can exclude employees that have been with the corporation less than two years
  - The company can exclude employees deemed "part-time"
  - The company can choose to exclude "highly compensated" employees
- The plan requires shareholder approval
- Any employee owning five percent or more of stock in the company is prohibited from participation in this type of program
- All employees are treated equally under the plan
  - The plan may provide a formula for purchase amounts based on a percentage of salary (similar to 401k plans)
  - The plan may provide a "ceiling," limiting the number of shares any employee can purchase
- The purchase price cannot offer more than a 15 percent discount from the fair market value of the stock on the date of grant or exercise
- The offering period is a maximum of 27 months if the "look-back" provision is invoked; if the purchase price is always determined on the date of exercise, the offering period can be as long as five years before new shareholder approval is required
- Employees cannot buy more than $25,000 in company stock through this type of plan in any one calendar year (not to be confused with a twelve-month period)

gains tax (20 percent) treatment on the *nondiscounted* portion of the employee's profit (see Table 3.2 for an illustration).

If the employee does not meet the holding period requirements and sells the stock in a "disqualifying disposition," the employee will incur ordinary compensation income (similar to NQSOs). While this income should be reported on an employee's W-2, very few

Table 3.2. Employee Stock Purchase Plans, *Qualifying* Disposition

Stock Price Assumptions (per share)		Tax Consequences (per share)	
FMV of company stock on date offering period begins:	$20.00	Ordinary income due on discount element: ($3 x 28% tax bracket = $0.84)	$ 0.84
FMV of company stock on date of purchase:	$40.00	Long-term capital gain: Sale price less the discount equals the basis for calculating:	$ 5.60
Discounted purchase price: ($20 x .85 = $17 per share)	$17.00	($48 – $3 = $45) Basis less the purchase price equals taxable amount	
Sale price:	$48.00	($45 – $17 = $28)	
Gain (loss):	$31.00	Taxable amount times 20% equals tax per share due: ($28 x 20% = $5.60)	

employers have systems in place to handle the withholding associated with this situation and the employee must recognize his or her tax liability and be prepared to meet that obligation (see Table 3.3 for an illustration).

While qualified (also referred to as Section 423 plans) ESPP programs are the most popular, some companies offer nonqualified programs that simply allow employees to save money through payroll deductions and purchase stock in the company. Because these plans are not qualified—meaning that they do not adhere to the rules and regulations of Section 423 or offer the possibility of favorable tax treatment to the employee—any gain the employee realizes at the time he or she purchases the stock (as a result of discount or price appreciation in the stock due to a "look-back" provision) is subject to ordinary income tax treatment.

ESPP programs also have a shorter life span than do most stock option plans. The typical option grant is for 10 years; most ESPP programs have an offering period that does not exceed 24 months. It is not uncommon for a company to seek shareholder approval on a

Table 3.3. Employee Stock Purchase Plans, *Disqualifying* Disp......

Stock Price Assumptions (per share)		Tax Consequences (per share)	
FMV of company stock on date offering period begins:	$20.00	Ordinary income due on FMV of company stock on date of purchase less the purchase price paid: ($40 – $17 = $23; $23 × 28% tax bracket = $6.44)	$ 6.44
FMV of company stock on date of purchase:	$40.00		
Discounted purchase price: ($20 x .85 = $17 per share)	$17.00	Capital gain: Sale price less ordinary income less purchase price: ($48 – $23 = $25, $25 – $17 = $8)	$ 2.24
Sale price:	$48.00		
Gain (loss):	$31.00	Taxable amount times tax rate ($8 × 28% tax bracket = $2.24)	

new ESPP program so that the transition from one program to the next is somewhat seamless, but the fact remains that they are different and unique programs and may have slightly different rules and requirements.

Restricted Stock Plan

A restricted stock plan (RSP) is a true hybrid: It is an actual stock bonus that is taxed as if it were a cash bonus (meaning that the "spread" between the grant price and the market price on the day the vesting restrictions expire is subject to payroll and ordinary income taxation).

Unlike NQSOs and ISOs, restricted stock awards are not options; they are an outright grant of company stock, subject to vesting restrictions. In other words, the company gives an employee, often management or executive level personnel, shares in the company and then requires that the employee work for a specified number of years before he or she can collect 100 percent of those shares (often referred to as "golden handcuffs").

The main benefit of these awards is that they do not require cash out of pocket as do stock option programs and ESPPs do; the drawback is that the vesting schedule dictates the payroll and income tax consequences (unless the employee utilizes an 83(b) election, which will be covered in detail later in the book). Figures 3.18 through 3.23 outline the potential tax consequences of RSP compensation.

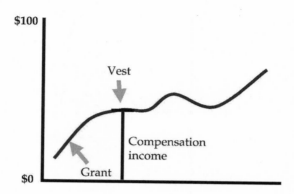

Figure 3.18 RSPs. (© Net Worth Strategies, Inc. 2002)

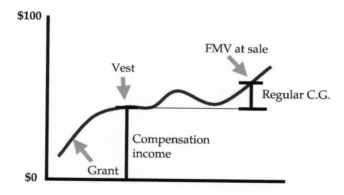

Figure 3.19 RSPs. (© Net Worth Strategies, Inc. 2002)

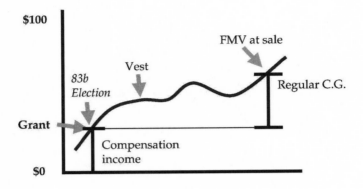

Figure 3.20 RSPs. 83(b) consequences. (© Net Worth Strategies, Inc. 2002)

- Example
  - Joe Client is granted 10,000 RSPs when FMV of stock is $10
  - Purchase price is $0
  - Shares vest 100 percent in three years and are sold immediately when FMV of stock is $50
  - Tax effects at grant:

	No 83(b)	Elected 83(b)
Number of shares granted	10,000	10,000
FMV of stock at grant	$ 10	$ 10
Ordinary income	$ 0	100,000
Combined ordinary tax rate	45.82%	45.82%
Tax liability at grant	$ 0	45,820

Figure 3.21 RSPs. (© Net Worth Strategies, Inc. 2002)

- Example cont'd
  - Tax effects from vest:

	No 83(b)	Elected 83(b)
Number of shares vesting	10,000	10,000
FMV of stock at vest	$ 50	$ 50
Ordinary income	$ 500,000	0
Combined ordinary tax rate	45.82%	45.82%
Tax liability at vest	$ 229,100	0

Figure 3.22 RSPs. (© Net Worth Strategies, Inc. 2002)

- Example cont'd
  - Tax and cash flow effects from sale:

	No 83(b)	Elected 83(b)
Number of shares sold	10,000	10,000
FMV of stock	$ 50	$ 50
Gross cash inflow	$ 500,000	500,000
Cost basis	$ (500,000)	(50,000)
Long-term capital gain	$ 0	450,000
Capital gains tax rate	20%	20%
Capital gains tax	$ 0	90,000
Prior taxes paid	$ 229,100	45,820
Total net cash	$ 270,900	364,180

Figure 3.23 RSPs. (© Net Worth Strategies, Inc. 2002)

RSPs are securities that also may be subject to special restrictions—under Rule 144—imposed by the SEC. This rule prohibits certain individuals from selling stock in the public marketplace unless they comply with its provisions.

Rule 144 was designed to support the Securities Act of 1933, which was intended to "provide full and fair disclosure of the character of the securities sold in interstate commerce and through the mails, and to prevent fraud in the sale thereof." Intended as a method for ensuring that the public has current information regarding a particular company, Rule 144 provides visibility in regard to the transactions of individuals deemed to be influential within the company. This classification usually pertains to what the SEC defines as control persons: directors, executive officers on the board, and/or any shareholder who owns 10 percent or more of the company's stock.

Control persons—insiders—are the substantial shareholders of corporations or those who are "in the know" regarding company operations. Insiders must follow a certain process to sell their shares and are limited in terms of the number of shares they can sell in any three-month period. All these rules and regulations were designed with the smaller shareholder in mind. Can you imagine what would happen to a company's stock if a 51 percent shareholder decided to sell all his or her shares in a single day?

In most cases, the company grants an employee restricted shares—complete with voting rights (unlike NQSOs and ISOs)—subject to a vesting schedule. As was indicated above, the employee does not have to pay to exercise restricted stock grants. Each time employees "vest" in shares, the restrictions are lifted and the shares are subject to payroll (Social Security and Medicare) and ordinary income taxes.

There are three basic requirements that must be met to sell securities under Rule 144:

1. The seller must file a Form 144 with the SEC and file a copy with the exchange where the security is traded (New York Stock Exchange, NASDAQ, etc.) either on the day of sale or one day before it.

2.   The stock must be held (meaning it was purchased through a typical brokered transaction) for one year.
3.   The seller is limited in terms of the amount of restricted stock he or she can sell within a three-month period. That limit is the greater of:
     • The four-week average weekly trading volume preceding the sell instructions *or*
     • One percent of the outstanding shares for the company

Refer back to Figures 3.1, 3.2, and 3.3, which outline the various tax consequences associated with different equity compensation awards.

Once you know which type of option you've been granted, you can begin to formulate a game plan to determine what you should do with them. Unfortunately, many employees subject themselves to the worst-case scenario through ignorance and neglect. Read on to further understand the complexities of option compensation and make sense of their potential value.

Chapter Checklist

• Know what type(s) of option(s) you've earned.
• Recognize that exercising your option or vesting in your stock—realizing ownership of that compensation—will have a variety of tax consequences, depending on when you exercise or vest and when you sell the actual stock:
     • NQSOs:
          • There are no tax consequences at grant or vesting.
          • Spread between the strike price and the market price on the day of exercise is subject to payroll and ordinary income taxes.
          • If it is held after the date of exercise, it is subject to capital gains taxes, depending on the length of time the stock is owned.
     • ISOs:
          • There are no tax consequences at grant or vesting.

- No regular income tax is due upon exercise, but the spread may be subject to the alternative minimum tax.
- If the stock is sold within the calendar year of exercise (disqualifying disposition) or before holding period requirements are met (one year and one day from exercise and two years from date of grant), the spread will be subject to payroll and ordinary income taxes.
- If holding period requirements are met, the spread between the strike price and the market price on the date of sale is subject to capital gains tax.
- ESPPs:
  - The bargain element is subject to payroll and ordinary income taxes.
  - The nondiscounted portion of the spread between the purchase price and the market price on the date of sale will be subject to capital gains taxes, depending on the length of the time the stock is owned.
- RSPs:
  - There are no tax consequences at the date of grant unless an 83(b) election is made.
  - The spread between the strike price and the market price on the day of vesting is subject to payroll and ordinary income taxes.
  - If it is held after the date of exercise, the spread is subject to capital gains taxes, depending on the length of time the stock is owned.

4

WHAT ARE YOUR OPTIONS REALLY WORTH?

This chapter acquaints you with the complexities and common mistakes associated with valuing your stock options. You will begin to appreciate the attention to detail that is required for accurately calculating the true worth your equity compensation represents.

As employees, we often suffer from unrealistic expectations.

Perhaps you've recently received a personalized annual statement from the human resources department, combining your total compensation and benefits to provide you with the "true value" of your position with the company. It's quite impressive when you add everything up. Too bad it isn't real! Small things like taxes, vesting schedules, and exercise and transaction costs somehow didn't make it into the final calculation. Funny how those little details add up.

Busy professionals glance at the top line of the report and conclude that things are looking pretty good and it's probably okay to splurge on a house or a car or an expensive vacation. But these successful professionals do a double take when they look at the bottom line and realize that less than 30 percent of what they thought their stock option proceeds would be actually gets deposited into their bank accounts. To avoid those kinds of expensive mistakes, let's look at a very simple approach—the "take home" formula—for calculating the value of your stock options. Figure 4.1 shows the simple calculation for determining the value you will realize from your equity compensation.

Let's look at a real-world situation so that you can see this formula in action.

Jill had worked for BIG Company for the last eight years and was awarded 1,000 nonqualified stock options three years ago. She had been promoted twice and was feeling pretty good about her future at BIG. Jill wanted to redecorate her house and pay off her car, and so she decided to exercise some of the options she'd been granted as a way to finance her goals.

BIG options came with a four-year vesting schedule, and so she was vested in 75 percent of her equity compensation, or 750 shares. Jill's grant price was $18, and her company's stock was currently trading at $27 [fair market value (FMV)]. Doing the "quick math" and comparing it to the recent human resources summary of benefits report, Jill figured she had $20,250 coming from her options (750 shares at $27). She knew there would be some transaction fees but figured she'd have about $18,000 to work with in terms of her house and her car.

Poor Jill! If she'd only known about the "take home" formula:

Take Home Formula

Beginning Value
(# vested options x market price)

    – Cost of Exercising
    (# vested options x grant price)
    – Brokerage Fees
    (commissions and margin fees)

Realized Value

    – Taxes

Take Home Value

Notice the calculation considers your VESTED options only. This is an important principle in terms of understanding your true "take home value". Your VESTED options are the only options you can benefit from at the moment. That's not to suggest you should ignore your unvested equity compensation, but for the purpose of planning to exercise and realize your gain, you must focus on what can drop to your bottom line.

It's fun to play "what if" games, but don't get caught in the trap of banking on paper wealth you can't actually realize when computing your "take home" value.

Figure 4.1 Take home formula.

Fair Market value	= 750 shares	×	$27.00 (FMV)	=	$20,250
Cost to exercise	= 750 shares	×	$18.00 (grant price)	=	–$13,500
Brokerage fees	= 750 shares	×	$00.10 (commission)	=	–$75
Realized value	=				$6,675
Payroll taxes	=	(6.2% Social Security, 1.45% Medicare applied to the spread)			– $516
Income taxes	=	(assume 28% bracket)			– $1,890
Take home value	=				$4,269

You are beginning to understand why many employees do a double take when they receive the actual proceeds from exercising their options. This is called a take home formula because it projects what you'll actually get to put in your pocket.

This simplistic approach doesn't account for every nickel and dime associated with exercising options. In Jill's case, for example, it does not factor in the margin expense she owes her broker for executing a "cashless exercise" or fees for wiring money to her bank account. Most brokerage firms offer a margin agreement that allows the investor to borrow money at a specified interest rate up to a certain level (usually 50 percent of the value of the investment portfolio). Margin can be very useful in a variety of exercise strategies that will be discussed later in the book.

If Jill had exercised *incentive stock options* and had held the shares long enough to qualify for preferential tax treatment (more on that in Chapter 5), the taxes for this formula would be calculated differently:

Fair Market value	=	750 shares	×	$27.00 (FMV)	=	$20,250
Cost to exercise	=	750 shares	×	$18.00 (grant price)	=	−$13,500
Brokerage fees	=	750 shares	×	$00.10 (commission)	=	−$75
Realized value	=					$6,675
Long-term capital gains taxes (20%)						− $1,350
Take home value	=					$5,325

In our example we assumed that Jill paid the taxes upon receipt of her stock option proceeds. Depending on her circumstances, the tax liability could be lurking in the shadows of the future. Jill may have received a check from her broker for over $6,675 and

1. Bounced her mortgage payment because her company took the payroll taxes out of her next paycheck and she wasn't planning on that shortfall.
2. Had to cancel her trip to Cancun because she didn't know she had to set aside extra cash to pay the IRS until her accountant prepared her annual tax return (most companies assume a 28 percent income tax calculation; what if her income tax bracket is higher and because of exercising her options they didn't withhold enough?).

We also calculated Jill's actual value based on a current market value of $27 per share. As the market price changes, so do all the values in the simple formula except the cost of exercising; the grant price remains the same until the option expires.

So what started out as a great idea—paying for her home improvements and her car—caused a great deal of confusion and frustration. Is it any wonder that employees like Jill end up thinking their stock options aren't quite as lucrative as they thought?

Let's reframe this scenario.

If Jill had just won $4,269 at a Las Vegas blackjack table, she'd be ecstatic. She wouldn't be calculating the cost of the plane ticket and the hotel room for Sin City; she'd be boasting of her good luck and telling everyone she won almost $4,300.

Stock option recipients experience the heartache and disappointment of expectations, not bank account. The take-home formula will help you keep your feet on the ground and estimate more realistically.

Chapter 5 deals with the most expensive aspect of equity compensation, that pesky relative who always seems to be picking your pockets and minimizing your take-home total—Uncle Sam.

Chapter Checklist

The variables that ultimately will influence what you take home from your stock option compensation include those you can influence and control and those you cannot:

- The grant price (which you cannot control).
- The FMV price of the stock on the day you exercise your option (which you can control in terms of timing).
- The "costs" associated with exercising and taking ownership of your company stock:
  - Paying the grant price (you can control this only to the extent that you can choose the number of shares you decide to exercise).
  - Paying the brokerage commissions (if your company allows you to work with a variety of brokerage firms, you can seek the

most competitive price per share; if you are required to work
with a specific brokerage firm, you cannot control this variable).

- Paying the margin agreement fees (this will be determined by
the brokerage firm you work with).
- Paying the applicable taxes (you control this by deciding when
to exercise your options and how many shares you will exercise
in a given calendar year).

5

UNCLE SAM...YOUR WEALTHIEST RELATIVE

This chapter educates you in an area over which you may have some influence and control as it relates to your equity compensation—taxes. Understanding the multiple layers of taxation to which you could be subjected will allow you to develop strategies and tactics related to the timing of your exercise activity and the subsequent sale of your company stock.

We have become a "contented constituency," enjoying the rewards of low inflation, low unemployment, rising wages, and an appreciating stock market—at least in historical terms. Our relative prosperity has insulated us from the creeping complexity of our tax code and left us all but oblivious to our eroding ability to accumulate and keep individual wealth. We resemble the frogs in the proverbial pot that don't realize the water has reached a boiling point until it's too late.

The fact is that employee stock options represent the most complicated form of compensation extended to today's workforce.

Tax Facts

Major tax code changes since 1954:

32

Increase in number of words in the tax code since 1954:

1,261,000

Complexity of Form 1040 (used by 56 percent of U.S. taxpayers):

- 79 lines
- 144 pages of instruction
- 11 schedules
- 19 worksheets

Percentage of taxpayers paying for professional assistance in preparing their returns:

55%

Source: Robert L. Bartley,
Wall Street Journal,
November 5, 2001.

Receiving stock options has forever changed your status as a taxpayer.

You've relinquished your limited role in the tax preparation process. Before you received stock options, you could confidently provide your records and receipts to your accountant (or cruise through your do-it-yourself tax-preparation software), spend 30 minutes reviewing the return, sign it, and send it in.

Those days are over.

You owe it to yourself and those you care about to understand the consequences of this form of compensation because it isn't necessarily a "zero-sum" game. Failing to understand the tax consequences of your stock option compensation, coupled with poor planning, doesn't mean losing just the value of your option grants; it could mean having to pay thousands, hundreds of thousands, and in some circumstances, millions of dollars in taxes and penalties without ever realizing the gain of that intended compensation.

But beware of letting the tax tail wag the dog! Minimizing taxes should not be your overriding priority. Maximizing what you actually put in your pocket as it relates to the equity compensation you've earned should guide your actions.

Taxes We Pay

Robert L. Bartley, in his *Wall Street Journal* article entitled "Time for Honesty in Taxation" (Monday, November 5, 2001) wrote that, "a complex tax code is political camouflage. Politicians keep inventing complexities to disguise the level of taxation."

In the Last 10 Years You've Spent

47 days participating in sporting and recreational activities*

58 days participating in hobbies*

146 days socializing*

3.2 years working to pay taxes†

> * Source: Americans' Use
> of Time Project, University
> of Maryland, December
> 1997.
>
> † Source: Tax Foundation,
> April 14, 2000.

As successful professionals, many of us assume that we have a basic
understanding of the taxes we are subject to; unfortunately, we
typically underestimate how much the IRS pockets from our income
sources and consistently overestimate how much money we actually
have at our disposal.

Following are a few facts that professional coaches Laura Hess
and Philip Cohen of SPARCK International shared in their April 15,
2002, weekly e-mail broadcast (*Source*: http//www.freedom.gov/tax-
cut/taxfacts.asp):

1. The average family today pays more in taxes than it spends on
    food, clothing, shelter, and transportation combined.
2. The Census Bureau reports that the average household pays
    $9,445 in federal income taxes alone, twice what it paid in 1985.
3. The average tax rate for the 437,036 individual returns filed for
    1916 was 2.75 percent.
4. Federal taxes consume about 21 percent of national income, the
    highest proportion since World War II.

5. Total taxes from all levels of government—federal, state, and local taxes—stand at a record 32 percent of national income.
6. The average family in 1998 worked 2 hours and 50 minutes every 8-hour workday to pay taxes. Most of that time—1 hour and 55 minutes—was spent working to pay federal taxes.
7. Tax Freedom Day, the day Americans stop working for the government and begin working for their families, fell on May 10 in 2001, the latest day ever (in 1950, Tax Freedom Day was April 3).
8. Over the course of President Clinton's administration, federal taxes grew by over 54 percent, rising from $1.154 trillion in 1993 to $1.784 trillion in 1999.

Taxing Trend

This year the average taxpayer spends 28 hours and 6 minutes on the Form 1040 and common schedules, a 40% increase since 1997. Overall, Americans toil for 6.1 billion hours each year preparing and filing taxes, accounting for 80% of the federal government's paperwork burden. The Internal Revenue Code has grown from 500 pages in 1939 to more than 7,600 pages today. When IRS regulations, court cases and other support material are added, the total is more than 47,000 pages. In comparison, Webster's Unabridged Dictionary, which contains definitions for every word in the English language, is only 2,783 pages.

Americans desperately need Tax Code simplification. It has gotten so bad that even the IRS does not understand it. According to the Treasury Inspector General for Tax Administration, government auditors who called the IRS's "tax help line' last year got incorrect or incomplete answers to their questions 47% of the time.

—ERIC V. SCHLECT,
National Taxpayers Union
Source: *Forbes*, May 13,
2002.

Following is an overview of the taxes that can affect you as a recipient of stock option compensation.

Payroll Taxes

Because these taxes are removed before a payroll check is deposited in the bank, we may not be fully aware of their impact and forget to factor them into the total tax bill. In 2003, you pay 6.2% of the first $87,300 you earned in Social Security taxes (a maximum liability of $5,412.60) and 1.45 percent on all of your wages for Medicare. Few of us realize we also pay payroll taxes on our contributions to qualified retirement accounts such as a 401k; we avoid income taxes on those contributions, but not payroll taxes.

Exercising stock options for the first time serves as a rude awakening for many employees as it relates to payroll taxes.

Whenever a stock option is characterized as compensation (100 percent of nonqualified options, 100 percent of restricted stock options, the discount element of employee stock purchase plan shares, and any employee stock purchase and incentive stock options that are sold "early," in effect a disqualifying disposition), you are subject to payroll taxes on that exercise activity. But not all companies withhold payroll taxes on ESPP and ISO "early" exercise activities, so don't assume that your tax liability will be taken care of automatically by your employer.

The problem is that since you were paid in stock as opposed to cash, the company has to decide how to be reimbursed for those taxes. Some corporations have agreements with brokerage companies that allow for those taxes to be subtracted from the transaction activity related to the exercise and rerouted back to the employer; other companies simply assess those taxes from your normal salary (making that next payroll check look a bit "skimpy") or require you to write them a check. The fact is, those taxes will need to be paid and you need to understand the cash flow consequences of each exercise activity.

Income Taxes

Once you establish your total income—the sum of your household wages, interest, dividends, business and/or partnership income, alimony, lottery and gambling winnings and the like—you can subtract all allowable deductions and determine your taxable income.

Once you have arrived at your taxable income, you simply apply the corresponding tax rates (see Figure 5.1) to establish your income tax liability. Most people are subject to both federal and state income tax rates; some of us are lucky enough to live in places that don't impose a state income tax in addition to the federal tax.

Revised Tax Brackets*				
2000	28%	31%	36%	39.6%
2001	27.5%	30.5%	35.5%	39.1%
2002-2003	27%	30%	35%	38.6%
2004-2005	26%	29%	34%	37.6%
2006 and beyond	25%	28%	33%	35%

* Economic Growth & Tax Relief Reconciliation Act of 2001

Income Tax Brackets for 2002 (using table above)

Marrieds: If taxable income is

Not more than $12,000
Over $12,000 but not more than $46,700
Over $46,700 but not more than $112,850
Over $112,850 but not more than $171,950
Over $171,950 but not more than $307,050
Over $307,050

The tax is

10% of taxable income
$1,200 + 15% of excess over $12,000
$6,450 + 27% of excess over $46,700
$24,265.50 + 30% of excess over $112,850
$41,995.50 + 35% of excess over $171,950
$89,280.50 + 38.6% of excess over $307,050

Singles: If taxable income is

Not more than $6,000
Over $6,000 but not more than $27,950
Over $27,950 but not more than $67,700
Over $67,700 but not more than $141,250
Over $141,250 but not more than $307,050
Over $307,050

The tax is

10% of taxable income
$600 + 15% of excess over $6,000
$3,982 + 27% of excess over $27,950
$14,625 + 30% of excess over $67,700
$36,690 + 35% of excess over $141,250
$94,720 + 38.6% of excess over $307,050

Head of Household: If income is

Not more than $10,000
Over $10,000 but not more than $37,450
Over $37,450 but not more than $96,700
Over $96,700 but not more than $156,600
Over $156,600 but not more than $307,050
Over $307,050

The tax is

10% of taxable income
$1000 + 15% of excess over $10,000
$5,117.50 + 27% of excess over $37,450
$21,115 + 30% of excess over $96,670
$39,095 + 35% of excess over $156,600
$91,742.50 + 38.6% of excess over $307,050

Figure 5.1 Tax brackets.

One of the most common areas of misunderstanding regarding the regular income tax system is that it's graduated. There are different levels of taxation in the computation of your total tax, meaning that you apply the lowest tax rates to your total income, the next lowest rate to the income that exceeds the ceiling on the lowest bracket, and so on. As an example, your income level may expose you to the 31 percent tax bracket, but that doesn't mean you pay 31 percent on 100 percent of your income; you pay that rate only on the amount of income that wasn't taxed at the lower levels. In effect, you are paying a significantly lower, blended rate.

The federal tax rates are scheduled to decline over the next several years, but as with all tax laws, this is subject to another legislative initiative that can change the rules as we know them.

As with payroll taxes, whenever a stock option is characterized as compensation (100 percent of nonqualified options, 100 percent of restricted stock options, the discount element of employee stock purchase plan shares, and any employee stock purchase and incentive stock options that are sold "early," in effect a disqualifying disposition), you are subject to income taxes on that exercise activity.

Many companies automatically withhold 28 percent of the proceeds of nonqualified and restricted stock option exercise proceeds, but the very act of exercising your options may catapult part of your income into another tax bracket (or two), and your employer's withholding policy may not meet your tax obligation when April 15 rolls around.

Most companies do not, however, have systems in place to withhold income taxes for the exercise and early sale of your company's stock (meaning that you decide not to hold out for the preferential tax treatment) related to ISOs and ESPPs. In those instances you and/or your tax consultant are left to piece together the total tax puzzle for your household circumstances the year you elect to make those transactions.

You now begin to appreciate the importance of cash management and tax planning as they relate to equity compensation.

Alternative Minimum Taxes

The year 2000 exposed the role incentive stock options play in subjecting individual taxpayers to the *alternative minimum tax* in an ugly and devastating fashion. The fact that many employees exercised incentive stock options at the height of a bull market and then failed to effect a disqualifying disposition before December 31, 2000, left them with enormous AMT liabilities (based on the spread between their strike price and the price of their company's stock on the date of exercise) and incredibly inadequate stock market value in their company stock to pay the tax bill (see Figure 5.2).

David Cay Johnson, a Pulitzer Prize–winning journalist, reported in a *New York Times* article that the Treasury Department indicates a 38 percent annual increase in those affected by AMT, estimating that the alternative tax will have affected 2.7 million taxpayers in 2002 and will involve as many as 35 million taxpayers by 2010.

Unknown to most taxpayers, we are subject to two tax systems every year: the regular tax system and the AMT system.

Enacted in 1969 and significantly modified as part of the Tax Reform Act of 1986, the AMT system was designed to close loopholes being used by "wealthy" taxpayers.

Congress enacted this tax because a handful of taxpayers with incomes exceeding $1 million paid no tax in 1967. Although changes in the tax code in 1969 virtually eliminated the deductions those taxpayers took advantage of, there was no repeal or revision of the alternative minimum tax section of the code at that time. Until 1990 the tax rate under the AMT calculation was no more than 21 percent. That rate was raised to 24 percent in 1990 and to the current rates of 26 percent/28 percent in 1993 as a way for Congress to project future revenue increases confidently.

Caught in the ATM Trap

Company	3/31/00 Closing*	3/30/01 Closing*	If a grant price of:	Taxable Spread/share
CMGI	$ 113.31	$ 2.54	$ 10.00	$ 103.31
PurchasePro.com	$ 36.25	$ 7.25	$ 2.00	$ 34.25
Level 3	$ 105.75	$ 17.38	$ 12.00	$ 93.75
Sun Microsystems	$ 46.85	$ 15.37	$ 7.00	$ 39.85
Microsoft	$ 106.25	$ 54.69	$ 43.00	$ 63.25

* Source: Maxxess History

Figure 5.2 Caught in the AMT trap.

AMT was not indexed for inflation, and so the tax-bracket creep that the "average" American worker has experienced since 1969 has resulted in more and more taxpayers being subjected to this tax. Every major tax law change compounds the problem (see Figure 5.3). The *National Taxpayer Advocate* suggests that a taxpayer may need an additional 12 hours just to file using the AMT method because of the complications of doing the calculation (Figure 5.4) and the deductions available under the regular tax computation method but not available under AMT.

1. Taxpayers exercise and hold stock options in order to pay 20% long-term capital gains tax at sale, but AMT forces them to instead pay 26% - 28% tax in advance of sale.

2. AMT credit can easily outlive a taxpayer, since it can be applied only to difference between successive years' AMT and regular income tax.

3. In a stock market downturn, the government's AMT collection is unaffected, while the stockholders' assets are decreased not only by the stock market loss, but also by the decimation of remaining stock and a lifetime of collected assets.

4. In a down market, even if you can somehow pay the tax from other assets, your real tax rate (low, middle or high class) remains incredibly high and can easily exceed 100%. And it is not certain that the stock will ever recover.

5. AMT drastically exacerbates the risk of holding for long-term capital gain.

6. The government does not pay interest on the collected AMT that generates a credit.

7. AMT collection, based on date-of-exercise unrealized gain, can be ultimately legitimized only in a bull market. In a bear market, the tax is unmasked as maverick to any other tax-collection process.

8. AMT causes gain from incentive stock options (which often substitute for salary) to be taxed in a disadvantageous manner.

9. AMT discourages the economically beneficial practice of holding stock.

10. AMT makes middle-class investment income unavailable.

11. The base income subject to AMT has not been adjusted for inflation in 32 years; therefore every year, this tax impacts increasing numbers of middle-income households.

12. Due to the complexity of AMT, tax experts and investment counselors are frequently either unable or unwilling to advise constituents about consequence of AMT, making AMT a major taxpayer hazard.

Figure 5.3 The 12 flaws of the alternative minimum tax. (Reprinted with permission from reformAMT.org.)

Why spend so much time learning about AMT? Because the exercise of ISOs is a preference item for the AMT formula and one of the "trigger events" that can subject you to the AMT calculation. If you exercise an incentive stock option, you should automatically calculate your tax liability according to the AMT computation as well as the regular tax method. You will be responsible for paying the higher tax calculated by the two different formulas.

In simple terms the AMT calculation can mean that employees pay a very real tax on a purely hypothetical gain. What is so maddening is that you are out of pocket for taxes without taking receipt of the gain. It's a paper profit that requires you to write a check to Uncle Sam.

There is a corresponding AMT credit that goes with this tax—you're basically providing the IRS with an interest-free loan—but there's no guarantee you'll fully realize that credit over time. Many of the unfortunate folks who exercised ISOs and found themselves faced with outrageous AMT liabilities for 2000 have no hope of exhausting their AMT credit during their lifetime.

How It Works

The alternative minimum tax gets its catchy name from the fact that this section of the tax code uses an *alternative* method for calculating your income tax.

You or your tax consultant plugs the data into the tax calculation software, and the program spits out two numbers: one number for your tax liability calculated according to the regular income tax rules and another number computed according to the alternative formula.

You pay the greater amount of the two.

The actual alternative calculation is complicated (i.e., certain deductions under the regular income tax formula—state income taxes, property taxes, interest on a second mortgage, and personal exemptions, to name a few—are not allowed, the standard deductions are different, etc.), making it difficult to predict when you will be subject to it.

But thanks to the 1986 tax law changes, exercising ISOs is one of the things that will cause you to calculate a higher tax liability using

Taxpayer advocate: Tax code too complex

Excerpts from an article
published Sunday, January 20, 2002
San Jose Mercury News
By Kathy Kristof

The U.S. tax code has become so complicated that millions of individuals can't even figure out how to properly report their family status and dependents, according to a report recently delivered to Congress.

And that's just one of the many problems the nation's 132 million taxpayers face today, largely as a result of unintended consequences of piling tax changes on top of one another over the years, Taxpayer Advocate Nina Olson said in a report delivered to Congress.

Among the problems:

... The alternative minimum tax, established to ensure that wealthy taxpayers paid at least some tax, which now hit individuals earning as little as $50,000 annually. Those who must figure their AMT liability – a group that now expanded to include virtually every middle- and upper-income family – can figure that filling a return will take an additional 12 hours. In most instances, taxpayers find that they don't owe AMT taxes, but that doesn't absolve them from doing a full day and a half of work.

Olson said her focus was not only to identify problems, but to talk about problems that could be solved. Much of what ails the current system could be fixed by simply eliminating the AMT for individuals and creating a single, uniform definition of "qualifying child".

Figure 5.4 Taxpayer advocate: tax code too complex.

the alternative formula. The spread between your stock option strike price and the fair market value of your company's stock on the day you exercise your option is an AMT adjustment item and part of that alternative calculation.

Alternative minimum taxable income is taxed at 26 percent (up to $175,000 in taxable income under the AMT formula) and 28 percent (over $175,000 in AMT income). There aren't any lower tax brackets to "soak up" as we're used to doing in the regular income tax schedule, and so this tax carries quite a "sticker shock" when it's delivered to an unsuspecting taxpayer.

If, however, you effect a "disqualifying disposition"—selling your company stock purchased through the exercise of an ISO before holding it for one year from the date of exercise and two years from the date of grant—prior to December 31 of the year in which you paid the strike price, you will trade your exposure to AMT for liabilities in the areas of payroll and ordinary income taxes, basically converting an ISO to an NQSO. The key to achieving this is selling before the end of the calendar year, not just within 12 months of holding the stock.

The "double tax whammy" would be selling in January of the year after exercise but before holding the stock for one year and one day, in essence triggering both AMT and compensation/ordinary income taxes.

And if you live in a state (such as California) that assesses a state AMT tax on top of the federal AMT calculation and have someone else prepare your taxes for you, this will mean more forms and fees added to the process.

AMT also increases your need to keep meticulous records. Suddenly your AMT liability affects your estimated taxes, the cost basis of the company stock you now own (you already paid taxes on the spread between the strike price and the fair market value on the day of exercise, and so you will now have a regular cost basis and an AMT cost basis), and the new AMT credit you may or may not be able to use to reduce the taxes you owe in future years. Obviously, this is something you should do with very competent and experienced professional assistance.

Capital Gains Taxes

Many of us are willing to take some calculated risks to trim our tax bills. The reason employees subjected themselves to the uncertainties of AMT in the past—besides being completely unaware that it existed—is that they were holding out for the possibility of a 20 percent long-term capital gains tax as opposed to 28 percent to 40 percent payroll and federal income tax.

When the stock market is appreciating, it's an attitude of "no harm, no foul." The dramatic market declines in 2000 and 2001 reacquainted

stors with the concept of volatility and market uncertainty
d some sobering circumstances that literally eliminated
capital gains and produced capital losses, leaving the uneducated
with big AMT liabilities and literally no stock market value to cash
in and settle the bill.

A capital gain (or loss) is related to the sale of what the IRS deems
a capital asset (something of lasting value such as a stock certificate
or a piece of real estate). The tax rates for long-term capital gains
offer some significant savings compared with ordinary income because the top rate is 20 percent. If you have a gain in a capital asset
you've held for one year and one day, you qualify for long-term
capital gains tax treatment, meaning the gain is taxed at a rate of 20
percent (unless you've held the asset for five years or longer, after
2001, which reduces the rate to 18 percent).

If you have a gain in the same asset but have not held it for one
year and one day, you have a short-term capital gain and will be
taxed at the same rates as those which apply to your ordinary income.

Capital gains tax is also easier to grasp because you actually realize
the gain (or loss) as a result of this transaction and have the liquidity
to meet your tax obligation, a luxury you may not have with
AMT. Long-term capital gains tax is more desirable because the
fixed rate of 20 percent looks quite attractive in contrast to the possibility of payroll taxes (7.65 percent), plus ordinary income taxes
(typically 27 to 38.6 percent for stock option recipients) and in some
instances state income taxes (3 to10 percent, depending on the state
in which you reside). No matter how you add it up, long-term capital gains tax looks pretty good in comparison.

This leads us to a little-known provision in the tax code that equity
compensation recipients should be aware of: the 83(b) election.

83(b) Election

The 83(b) election is a misunderstood provision in the tax code that
allows employees to accelerate their taxes in an effort to convert
payroll and ordinary income taxes into long-term capital gains
taxes. It is a strategy that comes into play in an early exercise circum-

stance, allowing the stock option recipient to take ownership of the stock for tax purposes but not for property purposes.

Used most frequently with restricted stock awards, this provision allows you to pay taxes early *as if you already owned the stock.* You calculate compensation income when you pay for the stock, taking constructive receipt, not when it vests. Theoretically, this allows you to recognize taxable income before substantial stock price appreciation in an effort to minimize your future tax liability.

You cannot make the 83(b) election for options (which is why it's most commonly used for restricted stock grants). This is a key point. If your plan permits—or does not specifically forbid—you to exercise your options before the vesting date, you can make the election for the stock you receive in an early exercise. You will pay for the stock, you will be taxed on the stock, but you won't actually own the stock until the vesting period expires.

You elect to accelerate the payment of tax although you have yet to meet the vesting requirement. This substantial risk of forfeiture—having paid the taxes prior to realizing the economic benefit of the property—is why the IRS allows you to make the election. If the stock becomes worthless or the market price falls below your exercise price or if you leave the employment of your company before vesting for any reason, you will have paid for stock you will not get and will have paid tax on income you didn't actually realize.

But in making this election, the optionee converts future payroll and ordinary income tax into capital gains tax, provided that he or she meets the requirement for the holding period. For many employees receiving restricted stock awards, this can mean a substantial tax savings and result in more money being realized from the equity compensation earned. For employees receiving ISOs, this election effects a disqualifying disposition—eliminating any AMT liability—and begins the capital gains clock with a new cost basis. And for employees in a private company before an initial public offering (IPO) who receive NQSOs, this can be an attractive strategy as it may allow you to minimize the compensation taxes and convert future appreciation in the stock price to long-term capital gains taxes.

This election must be done within 30 days of receiving the stock. It cannot be done upon receipt of an option, only upon receipt of the actual stock.

Now that we've reviewed the taxes we're most familiar with, it's time to turn to the real "success penalties" stock option recipients find themselves facing: estate taxes. Once reserved for the likes of Warren Buffett or Bill Gates, these taxes are sneaking up on people who would never consider themselves wealthy, let alone subject to the taxes of the superrich.

Estate Taxes

If you are the recipient of employee stock options, you need to do estate planning. Estate planning is an economic process that employs legal strategies and the corresponding documents that enforce them. It is not solely a legal process, a distinction many people fail to make.

We come into this world with nothing, but when we leave the earth forever, we do so with a lot of "stuff." Estate planning is about giving what you have, to whom you want, when you want, the way you want while avoiding any unnecessary taxes, court costs, or attorney's fees. And if you don't take the time to specify what should happen to your "stuff," the court system will do it for you.

Historically, the settlement costs of any estate range from 10 percent to 60 percent, depending on the level of assets and the planning that has been done. But estate taxes are the only section of the U.S. tax code that are 100 percent voluntary. These taxes are completely avoidable, but that requires thorough planning and attention to changing laws. Failure to plan for and use the various methods available for eliminating these taxes can result in your loved ones or intended heirs being subjected to the most aggressive taxes in the code.

Benjamin Franklin stated that we cannot avoid death or taxes. With a little bit of time and money, however, we can eliminate death taxes.

The Economic Growth and Tax Relief Recognition Act of 2001 has lulled many taxpayers into believing that their exposure to estate taxes will diminish over time and is "nothing to worry about." Quite the contrary! The revised tax system has three specific stages: relief, repeal, and resurrection:

Relief: The new law increases our individual unified transfer tax credit over the next several years (meaning we can pass on more wealth tax-free if we plan correctly).

Repeal: The new law eliminates estate taxes completely in 2010.

Resurrection: The new law has a sunset provision that literally puts the 2001 estate tax law back into force effective 2011, resurrecting the unified transfer tax credit of $1 million and taxing any wealth above that credit at rates of 37 to 55 percent.

At the time of death, your estate will include all your vested options whether you've exercised them or not. If you live in a community property state and your spouse dies before you do, 50 percent of your vested stock options will find their way into your spouse's taxable estate. Assuming that you and/or your spouse live until 2011 and then meet with an untimely demise, this is how these options will affect your estate:

Assets	Fair Market Value on Date of Death
House	$350,000
Investments	$450,000
Personal property	$100,000
Vested stock options	$375,000 (valued via the Black-Scholes method)
Taxable estate	$1,275,000
Unified transfer credit	–$1,000,000 (available only if planned for prior to death)
Subject to taxes	$ 275,000
Potential loss to heirs	$ 171,050 (combination of income and estate taxes; not subject to payroll taxes unless the exercise occurs in the same calendar year as the employee's death)

The lack of transferability of ISOs and the limited use of transferability regarding NQSOs make for some estate planning challenges. If stock options represent a sizable portion of your net worth, effective use of an advisory team (attorney, certified public accountant, financial planner) will be a necessity if your intention is to pass your hard-earned wealth to your family or to a charity. The U.S. tax code legislates that your stuff goes to the IRS, loved ones, or charity—you get to pick two of those three before your death.

Employee stock options can be a tremendous wealth-building tool, but they are not to be taken casually. Many people make the mistake of putting their stock option grants in a drawer and letting external circumstances dictate what happens next. This approach is costly; the money you will lose to the U.S tax code makes any advisory fees you incur while seeking good professional counsel look like pocket change.

Chapter Checklist

- Know the various layers of taxation you are subjected to as the recipient of stock option compensation:
  - Payroll taxes (Social Security and Medicare)
  - Income taxes
  - AMT taxes
  - Capital gains taxes
  - Estate taxes
- Know the rates of taxation associated with each type of tax:
  - Social security = 6.2 percent on the first $87,300 in 2003 income
  - Medicare = 1.45 percent on 100 percent of your wages
  - Income = see Figure 5.1 to identify your bracket and percent
  - AMT = 26 percent on the first $175,000 of AMT income, 28 percent on AMT income over $175,000
  - Capital gains = 20 percent on long-term holdings (one year and one day), your ordinary income bracket on short-term holdings
  - Estate = depends on the year of death and the unified credit available to apply to the value of the gross estate

6

THE NINE MOST COMMON MISTAKES TO AVOID WITH STOCK OPTIONS

This chapter identifies the common events that could cost employees money—unnecessarily—in relation to their stock option compensation. Most losses result from not anticipating the potential outcome of predictable planning circumstances. These situations and their consequences are typically identified in the company's stock option plan document and should be addressed as part of the formal planning process.

Many employees squander the wealth-building potential of their stock options because they are not proactive in their approach to managing the equity portion of their overall compensation. Instead, they react to circumstances as they arise and have to scramble to make the most of the situation without having much time to think things through.

The following external events drive most people's stock option activity:

- *Change of control*: The company announces it's merging with a competitor or acquiring another company.
- *Termination*: You decide you are going to quit and take another job or your position is eliminated and you are laid off.
- *Expiration*: Options that you received are about to expire.
- *Concentration*: More than 10 percent of your net worth is in stock options.
- *Disability*: A whitewater rafting trip puts you in a body cast for several months.
- *Division of marital assets*: You and your spouse have decided to divorce.
- *Death*: You meet with an untimely death.
- *Market timing*: Trying to guess whether the market will be up or down when exercising your options and ultimately selling your company stock.
- *Taxes*: Not considering the tax implications of your equity compensation.

Proper planning can anticipate each of these circumstances and insulate you from the erosion of wealth that occurs when you are forced to react to these situations if they occur.

Ideally, you would have an understanding of how your company's stock option plan document addresses each of these scenarios and put a strategy in place to address all these possibilities before they happen. The plan document will specifically address these issues and will govern the rules and timelines associated with each circumstance. Request a copy, read it, share it with your advisory team, and formulate a plan.

Let's examine each of these common events and some general guidelines for developing strategies that anticipate these events.

Change of Control

Merger and acquisition activity in today's economy rolls along at a pretty healthy pace. When companies the size of Chevron and Texaco can walk down the aisle of corporate matrimony, you have to accept the fact that virtually any company is subject to being bought by or joining forces with its nearest competitor.

Plan as if that were inevitable.

Your company's plan document should spell out what happens to your stock options if there is a merger, acquisition, or asset sale. Many times you will see language that allows for the *acceleration of vesting*—a clause that gives you an opportunity to exercise 100 percent of your options immediately as opposed to having to wait for the lapse of time outlined in your grant agreement—in the event of a change of control.

This is attractive because it allows you to realize the benefit of your stock option compensation earlier, but it has some significant tax consequences because you can't stretch that tax bite out over several tax years. Also, this opportunity is limited in scope: You may have less than 30 days to execute your exercise activity or lose it forever.

Real-World Example: Alice's Company Is Acquired

Alice worked for a successful mutual fund company that was acquired by a global insurance conglomerate. On the advice of her attorney, who insisted that deferring taxes as long as possible was the best strategy, she had never exercised any of her nonqualified employee stock options.

At notice of the acquisition she was given 15 days to exercise her vested stock options. She gave 53 percent of the value of those options to the IRS through payroll, state, and federal income taxes.

If Alice had exercised systematically beginning three years earlier (when the spreads between her strike prices and the market prices were actually lower), she would have pocketed 19 percent more of her stock option compensation because she would have paid less in taxes over that period of time.

You will have other investment and cash management decisions to make in this circumstance as well:

Will the shares you purchase in your current company convert to shares in the new, merged company?

Does the potential for price appreciation in that new stock make it worth holding for long term capital gains or are you better off exercising and selling simultaneously?

Will you receive stock options as part of your compensation package with the new company?

Could this merger result in the loss of your job? If so, what happens to your stock options?

Will you need the cash from this exercise activity to support your lifestyle until you find new employment?

Will the company withhold enough money from your exercise activity to meet your tax obligation, or do you need to reserve cash for that purpose?

In some situations, your company's plan document will state that there is no acceleration of vesting, and you will be faced with planning decisions related only to those shares in which you are vested. The bottom line is that you've earned a form of compensation that will be affected by any change of control affecting your company. Know ahead of time what those consequences are and what you will do in that situation.

Termination

If you sever your relationship with your company for any reason other than retirement, disability, or death, your plan document will specify the treatment of your stock option compensation.

Read this section of the plan document very carefully and make sure your understanding of the terminology matches that of the people administering the plan.

World Example: Randy's Severance Agreement

a midlevel manager, formerly an employee of a *Fortune 500* products company, met with his adviser in January to find out if he could exercise any of his stock options. Unfortunately, he had "missed his window" by 21 days, leaving $125,000 of "in-the-money" options with his former employer. How could something like this happen?

Randy's official termination date was September 19, but he received a severance package through December 31. The plan document allowed him to exercise his vested stock options for 90 days after termination, meaning that he had until December 19 to exercise his options. He confused the end of his severance period with his termination date, a costly and completely avoidable mistake.

If you are entertaining the idea of a job change, the impact that will have on your stock option compensation is an influential factor in your decision-making process. The standard "window" for exercising after termination is 90 days, but read your company's plan carefully for exceptions.

You need to understand what you are leaving behind so that you can negotiate appropriately for your next position. You also need to understand the mechanics associated with realizing the benefits of your vested stock options and implement the most tax-efficient strategy for exercising them, keeping more of what you've earned.

Expiration

Your employer has in effect given you a "use it or lose it" compensation coupon. You've earned the right to purchase a particular number of company shares, at a certain price, *within a specific period of time.*

There is a tendency, particularly with NQSOs, to delay any exercise activity until the last possible moment. That approach may or may not be aligned with your personal financial goals and may or may not coincide with your company's performance in the context of stock market cycles.

> Eleven percent of respondents allowed "in-the-money" options to expire unexercised.
>
> Source: Oppenheimer Funds Inc., May 2000 survey.

It is best to revisit the timing and pricing targets associated with your equity compensation *at least twice a year*. It is not uncommon for a combination of grants to be exercised concurrently in an effort to minimize taxes and maximize what you put in your pocket. Market conditions, strike prices, the number of vested shares, and your overall financial objectives should have more influence on the timing of your exercise strategy than does the fact that one particular grant is scheduled to expire in the very near future.

Real-World Example: Jack's Options Almost Expire

Jack, an executive with a popular beverage company, was letting his expiration date dictate his stock option compensation strategy. He literally ran down to a local Charles Schwab office three days before his grant was scheduled to expire and exercised his option so that he wouldn't lose it forever. Jack had had the grant 9 years and 362 days before he realized he needed to take action and was distraught because he had never exercised a single stock option he'd been granted (having received them annually for the last 10 years) and had no idea how the process worked.

This gentleman had the responsibility for developing strategic plans and their tactical execution for one of the largest brand franchises of the global economy, but he had no strategy for his equity compensation. He had passively let an expiration date determine the net result of a portion of his overall compensation package.

Since then Jack has adopted a systematic plan that allows him to straddle two tax years with each exercise over the next five years, managing the tax consequences of those options from a cash flow standpoint yet allowing him to exercise at particular pricing targets. This "reverse dollar-cost-averaging" program allows Jack to know exactly where the proceeds of each exercise will be invested and what role that will play in his overall wealth accumulation program.

Concentration

Conventional investment management wisdom advises against having too much of one's portfolio invested in a single company's stock. However, it's not unusual to find employees with 60 to 90 percent of their net worth tied up in their company's stock through a variety of programs: stock options and/or restricted stock, employee stock purchase plans, and company stock purchased or given to match salary deferrals through a 401k plan. The Enron debacle serves as the most visible reminder of the risks associated with having one's wealth concentrated in a single company's stock.

When Enron filed for bankruptcy during the fourth quarter of 2001, its employees lost over $1 billion in retirement savings as a direct result of investing in company stock. Investment professionals typically advise clients against having more than 10 to 15 percent of their investment assets in a single company's stock or a specific sector of the economy. Many of those who worked for Enron had 50 percent or more of their retirement savings tied up in company stock and watched a key component of their financial resources evaporate overnight.

Enron is not an anomaly or one of those once in a decade flukes. Figures 6.1 through 6.10 illustrate the fact that companies in industry sectors from high tech, to pharmaceuticals, to defense, to grocery stores are *not* immune to the volatility trumpeted in recent headlines. These are not exceptions; they are a very real part of the ongoing business cycle and should be regarded as the rule, not the exception. It's not a question of if this type of downturn will hit your company's stock, but a question of when and what you are doing to prepare yourself for the inevitable.

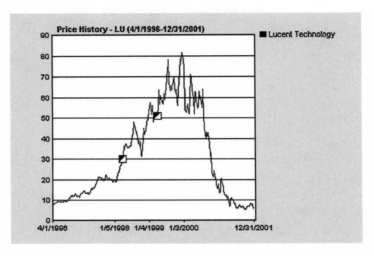

Figure 6.1 Who is this? An unusual case? (© Net Worth Strategies, Inc. 2002)

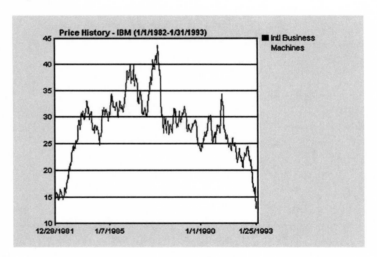

Figure 6.2 Other companies. (© Net Worth Strategies, Inc. 2002)

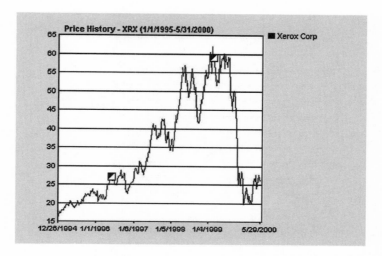

Figure 6.3 Other companies. (© Net Worth Strategies, Inc. 2002)

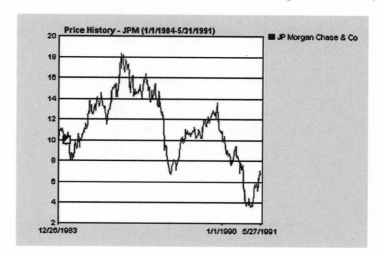

Figure 6.4 Other companies. (© Net Worth Strategies, Inc. 2002)

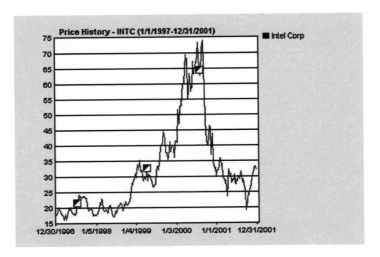

Figure 6.5 Other companies. (© Net Worth Strategies, Inc. 2002)

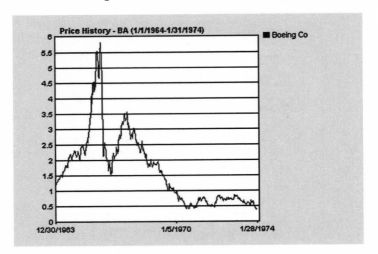

Figure 6.6 Other companies. (© Net Worth Strategies, Inc. 2002)

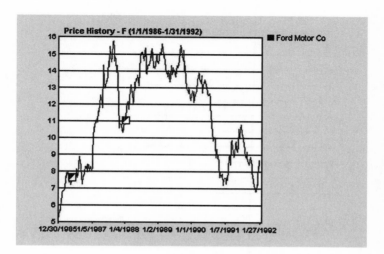

Figure 6.7 Other companies. (© Net Worth Strategies, Inc. 2002)

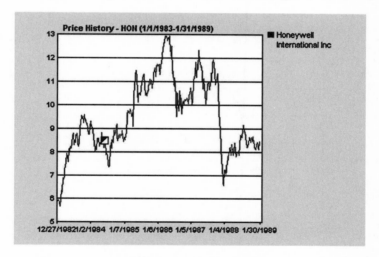

Figure 6.8 Other companies. (© Net Worth Strategies, Inc. 2002)

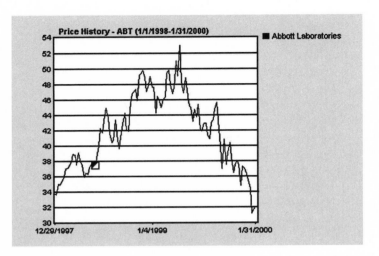

Figure 6.9 Other companies. (© Net Worth Strategies, Inc. 2002)

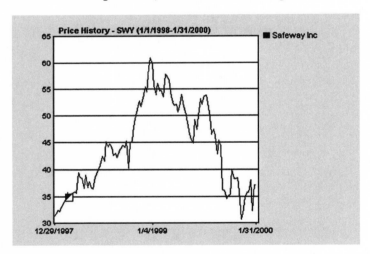

Figure 6.10 Other companies. (© Net Worth Strategies, Inc. 2002)

Stock option compensation quickly creates a condition of concentration and requires each recipient to pay particular attention to the risks that are compounded with each additional grant. How do you know if your wealth is too concentrated in a single company's stock? Answer a few questions developed by Dr. Donald Moine, an industrial psychologist specializing in compensation consulting:

1. How much are your home and other real estate holdings worth?
2. How much are your cars, boats, and other vehicles worth?
3. What is the rest of your stock portfolio worth (not including company stock or stock options)?
4. How much do you have in cash and CDs?
5. How much are your stock options plus any company stock you already own (in a regular brokerage account, in your 401k plan, through ESPP programs, etc.) worth?

If the answer to question 5 is more than the total for questions 1 through 4, your wealth is pretty concentrated and you are at risk of suffering a serious financial setback if there is a significant decline in your company's stock price.

Dr. Moine, president of the Association for Human Achievement, Inc., in Palos Verdes, California, would then ask, "Would you like free insurance to protect the value of your stock options and your company stock?"

Who wouldn't? You're already insuring your house and your cars because the cost of replacing them could be devastating. Those insurance premiums certainly aren't free; you're probably paying several thousands of dollars a year for that insurance. Dr. Moine specializes in a type of portfolio insurance known as cashless or zero-cost collars that you will learn about later in this chapter. Using cashless collars, you can protect tens of thousands to millions of dollars of your vested stock options and company stock at little or no cost. This free—or nearly free—insurance will protect one of the most sizable contributors to your overall net worth.

Following is a brief outline of some risk management strategies that can and should be considered if a significant part of your net worth (or potential net worth) consists of stock options and/or company stock.

- Diversify the investment portfolio.
  - "Unwind" the position in company stock over time and invest the proceeds in a variety of stocks and bonds and non-market-related investments to spread the risk and avoid putting all your eggs in one basket.
  - This is a reverse dollar-cost-averaging strategy that will systematically exercise and sell out of company stock over time.
  - This will eliminate any continued investment in company stock through 401k plans (if possible) and ESPP programs.
  - This is most appropriate for smaller stock option positions that might not qualify for some of the more sophisticated hedging strategies.
  - This takes time and still doesn't offer true security in the event of a significant decline in the company's stock price.
- Provide a hedge against a price decline.
  - Initiate the use of a protective option strategy that provides downside price protection:
    - You buy a put option (for several dollars per share), effectively establishing a "floor" price and protecting yourself from a stock price decline below that price.
    - The put gives you the right to sell your stock at any time during the length of the put contract (i.e., nine months) at the guaranteed floor price even if the stock price is trading well below the contracted floor price.
    - If the stock price is above the put contract price at expiration, the put will expire without value and you will lose the "premium" (the several dollars per share you paid) for that contract.
  - Initiate the use of an option strategy that provides current income and allows for participation with limited upside potential:
    - You sell a covered call option (for several dollars per share), effectively establishing a "ceiling" price and providing you with payment today for the value of those shares up to that price; this is the "premium" you receive.

- If the stock price is above the ceiling you set in selling the covered call at maturity, you forfeit the gains above and beyond the contracted price and may have to deliver your shares of stock upon completion of the contract.
- Initiate the use of a hybrid option strategy that combines the protective put and the covered call in what is referred to as the zero-premium collar or, in Dr. Moines's terms, the "free insurance":
  - You sell a covered call option and use the premium received to purchase a put option, creating a "collar" (because you've effectively hedged both your upside gain and your downside risk).
  - The maturity of the collar can range from several months to several years and can be designed so that both contracts mature simultaneously.
  - You are essentially gaining downside protection without paying an up front premium because you offset the expense of the put with the proceeds of the covered call, hence the term *zero-premium* collar (also referred to as a "cashless" collar).
  - Your risk in this strategy is the complete loss of the premium paid for the put, the forfeiture of any gain above the ceiling set in the covered call contract, and the possibility of having to physically deliver your stock certificates at maturity.
- Monetize the position to provide liquidity for other financial needs:
  - Initiate the use of a prepaid forward sale, a risk management strategy that allows you to monetize a concentrated equity position without incurring an immediate tax liability.
  - This strategy is most appropriate for investors who have restricted or unregistered (pre-IPO) shares or stock with a very low cost basis.
  - This allows you to effectively collateralize 75 to 95 percent of the value of your stock and/or options, realizing the liquidity of the majority of options without incurring the tax consequences, and diversify with the borrowed funds.
  - In structuring this strategy, you purchase a put option at 100 percent of the current stock price and sell a covered call option at 125 percent of the current price.

- As with a home equity loan, you put your capital asset—your stock options—at risk. At maturity, you may elect to settle the transaction by delivering stock or cash.

These are time-tested, sound strategies that are readily available but underutilized. You will need to work with an investment professional who is experienced in these areas as well as a tax adviser who can counsel you on the impact these strategies may have on your individual circumstances.

With tools like these available, why aren't more stock option recipients who find themselves with their personal wealth concentrated in company stock putting them to work?

Why would successful professionals be unwilling to recognize their exposure to the risk of significant loss and irreparable damage to their net worth?

Why would an otherwise savvy and intelligent person harbor unrealistic expectations regarding the performance of their company's stock in the equity markets?

Why would anyone jeopardize his or her financial future by betting on a single company's performance?

> Wharton professors David F. Larcker and Richard A. Lambert conducted research to determine the value employees place on stock options. Based on a survey conducted in March 2001, Larcker and Lambert concluded that *"the employees value their options more than they are theoretically worth."*

These things happen because stock option compensation from an employee's perspective is an emotional issue, not a financial issue. Emotions overtake intellectual capabilities to the detriment of the family financial objectives, and that's where some of the most costly mistakes are made.

Concentrated wealth is a compelling reason to seek professional help in managing your stock option compensation. Let someone who is not emotionally attached to your company's stock price evaluate the merits of your equity compensation on the basis of investment criteria, tax consequences, and the role your company's stock should play in your overall strategy for wealth accumulation.

Real-World Example: Microsoft and Enron

This following excerpt from an article, "How Losses to Enron Shareholders and Employees Could Have Been Minimized or Even Avoided," by Dr. Donald Moine, is reprinted with his permission.

> I have been able to collect some fascinating examples of the use of cashless collars that validates their power and effectiveness. Paul Allen, co-founder of Microsoft, used cashless collars to protect $1.7 billion of his Microsoft holdings at almost no cost. At least one senior executive at Global Crossing used cashless collars to protect several hundred million dollars of his holdings—again, at almost no cost.
>
> Incredible as it seems, sometimes people turn down the opportunity to use cashless collars. Why would someone turn down stock insurance? Think of someone who "knew" his house would never burn down or who "knew" he would never get in a car accident. That person would never buy homeowner's insurance or automobile insurance. If a corporate employee "knows" the value of his company's stock will never decline, or will only temporarily decline, why would he want protection from downside risk? I recently found a spectacular example of this type of thinking buried in a few lines of a *Wall Street Journal article*.
>
> The January 14, 2002, article, "Enron Ex-CEO Made Sideline Bet vs. Rival," detailed how Jeffrey Skilling made a multi-million-dollar bet that the stock of one of Enron's competitor's, AES, would decline in value. While he was sure the AES stock would drop in value, he apparently didn't think Enron stock would decline. Buried deep in the article is the mention that executives at Charles Schwab suggested Skilling use a collar to protect the value of his Enron holdings. Remember that a collar can often be structured so as to be cashless or free. Apparently the Schwab representatives were not very persuasive as Skilling turned them down on their offer to use a collar to protect the value of his 1.1 million Enron shares and 500,000 vested op-

tions. Big mistake. The collar could have saved Mr. Skilling more than $30 million. Incredible.

Like many other Enron executives, Jeffrey Skilling is now besieged with lawsuits. Had he engaged in this one transaction, he would be $30 million richer today. That is $30 million he could use for his defense, or to pay judgments, or to help Enron employees who now have worthless 401ks. It occurs to me that if some of the lawyers defending Skilling knew the significance of his turning down this offer to use a collar, they might be able to utilize this fact as proof of his total belief in Enron.

Disability

The plan document will govern the definition of disability and the time in which you (or your personal representative, depending on whether you have the appropriate legal documents in place and your employer accepts that individual as the legal equivalent of you) are allowed to exercise the options in which you are already vested. In many plans this will be one year from the date of termination of service.

The critical planning concern in the instance of disability is that your personal representative (most commonly a spouse or family member) understand the issues: what types of options you have, where the related documents are kept, how many shares you are vested in, how to execute the exercise of your options, and whom to contact to complete the process.

Real-World Example: John's Car Accident

Coming home from the office on a rainy night in Portland, John Weber was hit by a drunk driver. John survived the accident but was in a coma for almost seven months. His company did not offer short-term disability insurance, and so John's wife, Sara, scrambled to make ends meet until the long-term disability benefit from his company kicked in 90 days later.

John earned a base salary plus commissions in his sales position with the company, and his disability benefit replaced only 60 percent of his salary, not his total compensation. Sara, having quit her job after the birth of their second child, found herself racking up credit card debt at a record pace as she tried to figure out how to reduce expenses while wondering if John was ever going to recover from the accident. She remembered that John had recently passed the vesting date on some of the stock options he had been granted, and so she called the company to see if she could exercise the options and sell the shares in an effort to supplement the disability payments they were receiving.

Because the options were not transferable, the company's plan document prohibited Sara from exercising them. The stock plan administrator asked Sara if John had ever signed a financial power of attorney giving Sara the legal right to act on his behalf if he was not capable of acting for himself. Unfortunately, John and Sara had not created wills or trusts or powers of attorney for health care or finances. If John had signed such a power of attorney, the company would have allowed Sara to exercise the vested options and sell the resulting shares because that document would be the legal equivalent of John making those decisions and would not be considered a transfer.

John did recover and returned to work 20 months after his accident. John and Sara are still digging out from underneath the debt they incurred during his prolonged recovery but have increased his disability insurance coverage and put a living trust, with all the appropriate powers of attorney and guardianship language, in place.

Division of Marital Assets (Divorce)

Generally, unvested stock options are considered fair game in the process of dividing assets between divorcing spouses. Most jurisdictions (but not all) consider options property for marital distribution purposes because they are issued as a benefit of employment, the employee has a contractual right to exercise them, and many of the contingencies related to qualifying for this compensation benefit are perceived to be within the control of the employee.

> Stock option plans are not qualified plans. Therefore, "qualified domestic relations orders" (QDROs), which are required for the division of pension and other Employee Retirement Income Security Act (ERISA) assets, do not have any influence on these assets.

Vesting rules, expiration dates, and tax code treatment of stock options complicate the eventual outcome of divvying up these assets, but they have no bearing on whether stock options are subject to the divorce proceeding.

Stock acquired through the exercise of options is straightforward. It doesn't matter what type of options they were; you can make postdivorce, tax-free asset transfers as long as that is specified in the divorce property settlement. You will transfer the cost basis and corresponding holding period for tax purposes as well. Your former spouse assumes the tax liability with the stock.

Due to Revenue Ruling 2002-22, the IRS recently decided that a divorcee does not have to pay tax on the exercise of vested stock options that have been transferred to a former spouse when that former spouse exercises them. This represents a significant change from previous policy—the option holder (the company employee awarded the stock option) used to be taxed on the equity transferred to the ex-spouse, regardless of option type, prior to this change. In other words, the employee spouse transferred the asset (the option) to his or her former spouse but not the tax liabiability. This circumstance made for some very complicated planning issues. But the IRS concluded that the spouse receiving the options does have to pay tax on the exercise.

> A 1994 Louisiana case (Goodwyne vs. Goodwyne) involving "underwater" options (options that are trading below the strike price in the market place and, therefore, considered worthless) actually resulted in a postjudgment proceeding when the options later developed value.

Real World Example: The Taxing Realities of Divorce

Ned and Dierdra were divorcing after 16 years of marriage. Ned had been earning annual NQSO stock option grants for the last seven years in his sales management position with his company. Ned's total stock option holdings were worth approximately $500,000. Ned was only vested in options valued at $200,000 at the time of the divorce.

Dierdra's attorney argued that she was entitled to 50% of the vested stock option portfolio. Ned and his attorney found this logic reasonable and agreed to specific dates over the next three years for Ned to exercise his options and transfer the proceeds to Dierdra's investment account. Both Ned and Dierdra knew this approach put the value of this part of the settlement at risk due to the volatility of the stock market, but because there was no other way they could think of to divide the options equitably, they agreed to implement this plan.

After the three-year, systematic exercise strategy had been executed, Ned and Dierdra would have completed the division of their marital assets. Any stock option grants awarded to Ned after the final divorce decree (but before the three-year exercise strategy had been completed) would be considered the sole property of Ned, and Dierdra would make no claim against those awards. They agreed to these terms, signed the paperwork, and went their separate ways.

What Ned and Dierdra and their attorneys didn't understand is that they unknowingly reduced the total take home value of the stock options being divided in the divorce by adopting a "max tax" strategy.

In agreeing to have Ned exercise his options over a three-year period and split the net proceeds with Dierdra, both parties agreed to have the spouse in the highest tax bracket complete the transaction. As a result of the change in the tax law, both Ned and Dierdra would have realized more take home value by dividing the options, not the proceeds, and letting Dierdra exercise the options herself. Because Dierdra earned significantly less income than Ned (even with alimony figured into her total adjusted gross income), the total taxes due on the exercise of the options awarded to her as part of the divorce settlement would have been less, yielding more take home value for her. In addition, Ned would have the flexibility to exercise his options whenever it best suited his circumstances versus the three-year time frame dictated by the divorce decree.

If stock options represent a significant portion of your household's net worth and you find yourself divorcing your spouse, consider seeking the assistance of a Certified Divorce Planner (www.institutecdp.com). A family law attorney is a legal expert, not a financial expert. Stock option compensation is complicated, and divorce has incredible long-term financial implications that should not be underestimated.

Death

If an employee dies with vested stock options, the plan document will specify how long the estate's executor or heirs have to exercise those options, but the time frame will not exceed the term of the option agreement itself. In other words, if a vested option is scheduled to expire prior to the time the plan allows for exercise activity after death, the grant expiration date will have precedence.

Some plans provide for an immediate acceleration of vesting upon death; other plans stipulate that unvested options revert back to the plan. Some plans also accelerate the expiration dates associated with unexercised options in an attempt to limit the company's liability and reporting associated with deceased employees.

Many plan documents allow for a year from the date of death for exercise. Although all agreements provide for the transfer of options after the participant's (the option recipient's) death "pursuant to the will or the laws of descent and distribution," not all states provide for stock options to be transferred at death by way of beneficiary designation. Unfortunately, with a simple will in place, some states may take more than a year to complete the probate process. This circumstance can lead to frustration and asset evaporation as it relates to the equity compensation in the estate. Imagine having to calculate the worth of the unexercised options as part of the taxable estate and then not having the legal right to exercise those options and realize the value of those assets because matters are still being sorted out!

Real-World Example: Relying on the Kindness of Strangers

Patricia worked for a large drugstore retailer that offered a very progressive employee stock purchase plan. She had participated for several years and had amassed a nice little nest egg that she had earmarked for her children's college education. Unfortunately, Patricia didn't win her battle with breast cancer and never lived to see her children go to college.

Patricia and her husband had divorced several years before her death, and at that time Patricia had retitled her bank accounts to exclude her ex-husband and include her mother. Patricia's mother knew that if the proceeds of her daughter's stock purchases went to the children, they would end up being spent by the ex-husband (as the custodian of his minor children's assets) well before the first college tuition check was due.

Patricia's mother phoned the administrator for the company's ESPP plan and requested that the proceeds of the stock be transferred to the joint checking account that listed both Patricia and her mother on the account. The administrator, knowing Patricia's circumstances, "looked the other way" and transferred the money to the account. The administrator is quoted as saying, "I haven't checked with any lawyers and don't know if this is even legal; it just seems like the right thing to do."

Estate planning is mandatory for all stock option recipients.

The existence of stock options in any estate requires more immediate and detailed income tax planning than does any other type of asset held in the estate.

The type of stock options granted to the deceased and the state laws by which they are governed (community property, separate property, etc.) will determine the planning required.

What if the nonemployee spouse dies first and the couple lives in a community property state?

- Fifty percent of the value of the vested stock options is considered to be in the deceased spouse's estate.

- If non-pro-rata divisions *are specifically authorized* in the will or governing instrument, this will allow for a tax-free division of property.
- If non-pro-rata divisions are *not specifically authorized in the will,* the division may be treated as a taxable exchange or sale.

The point is that these are complicated assets to have in an estate and that you should address the consequences of an untimely death before it actually takes place.

No special income tax benefit is extended to the beneficiary of an unexercised NQSO. The "step-up" in cost basis typically associated with inherited assets does not apply in this situation. When the beneficiary exercises those vested NQSO options, the spread between the grant price and the market price will trigger ordinary income tax (but not payroll taxes) and is considered *income in respect of a decedent* [IRD], a fancy term associated with assets that have never been taxed before (like money in an individual retirement account [IRA] or 401k) and another detail to keep track of for an income tax deduction if estate taxes are due.

If the employee dies with vested ISOs, once again the value of those options will be included in the taxable estate. Unlike NQSOs, exercise of ISOs will not result in immediate taxation for the recipient and the beneficiary will receive a step-up in cost basis, effectively the market price on the date of death (or an alternative valuation date if applicable) plus the exercise price. The holding period for purposes of determining capital gains tax treatment begins on the date of exercise with the new, stepped-up cost basis.

Death will, however, remove all holding period requirements related to long-term capital gains status for ISOs *that were exercised prior to death.*

An AMT adjustment does occur for a beneficiary who exercises an ISO, but the AMT calculation is equal to the difference between the market price and the grant price on the date of exercise *plus the stepped-up option basis.*

This effectively reduces the AMT adjustment used for the tax calculation of the recipient. Because of this adjustment, any AMT credit due to the deceased employee (from previous ISO exercise activity and AMT liability) is not transferable to his or her estate.

Market Timing

As employees of the company in which we are buying stock, we tend to think we have the inside track on activity that will influence the market price of our stock. Unfortunately, there is a tendency on the part of employees to overemphasize the intrinsic value of their company's stock. While that kind of loyalty is part of the reason management institutes equity compensation programs, it can prove detrimental in terms of managing stock option compensation effectively.

Real-World Example: A Cloudy Crystal Ball

Bob had worked for his company for over two decades and had every intention of retiring from that company in another 10 or 12 years. He'd seen a few business cycles and weathered several restructuring initiatives, always impressed with management's ability to "bounce back."

On the advice of his broker, Bob decided to exercise some of his nonqualified stock options and begin to diversify his portfolio. But rather than execute the cashless exercise as was recommended, Bob decided to exercise and hold, "knowing"that the company's stock price was due for a little run-up in value.

On the date of exercise, the proceeds of Bob's stock sale would have been approximately $280,000. Within one month of exercising, the stock price had tumbled and Bob's portfolio value had dropped to $120,000. Confident that it would bounce back, Bob refused to sell the stock. Six months after his exercise activity his portfolio value had declined to $45,000, and one year later his company stock was worth only $11,000. To add insult to injury, Bob owed over $42,000 in income taxes (because the company withheld only 28 percent on his exercise activity and his taxes exceeded that rate) on his original exercise activity.

Investing in the stock market involves risk, and we are reminded of that on a daily basis. Taking your chips off the table after a winning hand is the only sure way of leaving as a winner, and the stock market isn't much different. Exercising and holding is a more common strategy for ISOs and can make sense, but establishing a "floor" for the share price and not letting emotions or taxes keep you from selling if the stock reaches that price point is an important part of realizing the value of your equity compensation. Effective market timing has eluded investors since Wall Street was established. Don't wager your stock options because you think you have a better "crystal ball."

Taxes

Ignorance regarding the tax consequences of equity compensation is often the most expensive mistake made by optionees. Stock options are a form of compensation and will therefore be subject to some form of taxation. When that compensation is taxed, and to what extent, is within your control. Unfortunately, too many employees do not realize their ability to influence the outcome until the damage is done. Understanding the layers of taxation is a critical first step in beginning to maximize your equity compensation.

Real-World Example: The True Cost of AMT (© Copyright 2001, 2002 ReformAMT)

Janine Valdivieso, age 44, grew up in southern California and now works as an office administrator in San Jose. She is married, has three daughters, and lives in a middle-class neighborhood. After they were married, Janine and her husband, Joe, began saving for college tuition for their two youngest daughters and setting aside money to buy stock for their retirement fund.

For most of her life Janine was a correctional officer for various government agencies. It wasn't until August 1999, when she was offered a job at Symyx, that she made the decision to enter the private domain. As a part of her overall offer, Janine was granted incentive stock options and, like many others, hoped they would offer her family a better financial future. She accepted a lower salary than she had wanted because her company offered her ISOs. Janine and her husband (who works for Sandisk) were told by their employers that they would not be affected by the alternative minimum tax (AMT), as long as they held on to the stock and did not sell during the same year, information that would prove to be both incorrect and financially devastating.

Janine and Joe followed that advice and purchased their shares as they vested throughout the year. One transaction in particular was especially damaging. The option or strike price was around $3, but the company stock trading on the market closed that day at $94. The alternative minimum tax is based on the difference between the price they paid for the options and the fair market value, or closing price, on that same day. By the end of the year, even though it was a paper profit only because they did not actually sell any of those shares, the Valdiviesos owed tax in the amount of $100,000 in addition to the almost $25,000 they paid throughout the year, an amount greater than their combined annual income. To pay it, they had to sell most of their stock at a much lower price than the price they were taxed on. They also had to sell all the stock in their retirement funds, and cash in the girls' college tuition savings.

"Our main concern right now is coming up with the funds to pay for our daughter's tuition at the state college next year," says Janine. "And we have to start all over on the retirement fund. It's not going to happen anytime soon."

Learn from the Experience of Others

None of us will live long enough to learn only from our own mistakes. If we're fortunate and pay close attention, we can gain insight from the experience of others and make ourselves aware of the pitfalls and potential hazards that lie ahead of us on the road of life. Don't let these common circumstances related to stock options dictate how much of your equity compensation you and your family will realize. Plan ahead and avoid unnecessary headaches, heartaches, and expenses. You earned those stock options and deserve to maximize the benefits they can provide. Don't leave your chips on the table.

Chapter Checklist

- Know what will happen to your stock options if there is a change of company in control.
- Know what will happen to your equity compensation if you quit or are laid off.
- Realize that you need to be proactive with regard to your stock option expiration dates and don't wait until the last minute to implement a strategy.
- Learn how to avoid having too much of your personal wealth tied up in company stock or stock options.
- Recognize the need to educate your spouse or another family member on the details related to your stock option compensation in case you are disabled and unable to act on your own behalf.
- Be aware of the pitfalls of dividing stock option compensation in a divorce and consider working with an attorney and a Certified Divorce Planner who can assist you in devising an appropriately fair settlement.
- Understand that your stock option compensation requires you to begin detailed estate planning to avoid the unnecessary erosion of wealth you've worked hard to create.
- Recognize that it's time in the market, not market timing, that has proved to be profitable over time.
- Realize that ignorance is an expensive luxury when it comes to understanding the layers of tax you may encounter as a result of your equity compensation and invest in your education in this area.

7

GRADUATING FROM AN EMPLOYEE TO AN OWNER

This chapter provides some guidelines for deciding how and when to exercise options. We examine a variety of exercise methods and some basic principles for determining when it may be appropriate to take ownership of company stock. We also discuss the administrative details related to the actual process of exercising and selling equity compensation.

You won't realize the benefit of your equity compensation until you exercise your options and actually take ownership of company stock. But taking ownership is a decision-making process that must balance the following considerations:

1. What will you do with the company stock once you own it, and why?
2. How will you pay to exercise your options?
3. What are the tax consequences of your decisions regarding questions 1 and 2, and how will you meet them?

How You Pay to Play

On the basis of the provisions for payment in your company's plan
document and your individual grant agreement, you have choices
regarding how you "pay to play" and actually become an owner of
your employer's stock. Most plans (but not all) allow for the following payment methods:

1. Cash:
    - The only exercise payment strategy for a pre-IPO company.
    - Not used very often by employees.
2. Promissory note:
    - The old-fashioned IOU.
    - Commonly used by senior executives (but under scrutiny in
      the post-Enron/MCI/Global Crossing/Tyco era).
    - Not available unless specifically stated in the plan document.
3. Stock swap:
    - Using previously owned shares as "currency" for payment.
      - Swapped shares:
        - Previously owned and surrendered to exercise a new
          option.
      - Replacement shares:
        - Shares received in a one-for-one exchange for swapped
          shares.
        - A tax-free exchange under Section 1036 of the code for
          an equal number of shares.
        - Carryover cost basis from the swapped shares (ISOs).
        - Substituted basis from the swapped shares (NQSOs).
      - Additional shares:
        - Shares received in excess of replacement shares, the
          compensation element of the swap.
        - Zero cost basis in additional shares received in the swap.
      - The holding period governing tax consequences on sub-
        sequent sale begins on the date of swap for ISOs; the
        holding period for NQSOs is "tacked on."
    - A notarized statement indicating certificate numbers to be
      swapped is recommended for record-keeping purposes.
4. Broker margin agreement:

- Technique for executing a "cashless exercise."
- You use credit extended by a brokerage firm to finance the purchase of your shares.
- Most common payment method for employees in publicly traded companies that allow for this process of payment.
- Not available for privately held companies (pre-IPO).
- Recommended specifically for exercising options but *not* for leveraging your investment portfolio and/or diversifying your investments.

Equity Compensation: Do I Want Stock or Cash?

Your decision to exercise your options should be made within the context of an overall financial plan. Exercising your stock options is not an isolated event and doesn't happen in a financial vacuum. Once you understand the type of options you have, the cash flow and/or investment implications of your decision to exercise and sell or hold the shares, and the corresponding tax consequences of your actions, you can proceed confidently in executing your strategy. Following are some general guidelines and principles to consider in exercising your options:

1. Exercise and sell (also called a same-day sale, most commonly a cashless transaction).
    - You exercise your options and sell 100 percent of the shares you purchase in a single transaction.
    - A savvy strategy for NQSOs:
      - NQSOs are considered compensation from a tax standpoint, and so you can "cash in" and eliminate the further market volatility and investment risk associated with a single stock position.
    - Using this method for ISOs results in a disqualifying disposition, effectively converting ISOs to NQSOs:
      - You sacrifice the possibility of achieving long-term capital gains status.
      - You avoid AMT liability if you transacted within the calendar year.

2. Sell to cover.
    • You exercise your options and sell just enough shares to cover the tax, brokerage, and margin fees associated with your exercise activity:
        • Review the assumptions regarding the tax calculation, as some plans and/or brokers use 28 percent across all employee stock option activity and you may need to set aside cash for a higher tax liability.
    • Particularly effective for NQSOs if you are interested in future stock swap strategies.
    • Often used for ISOs, particularly when you don't want to take cash "out of pocket" to exercise your options:
        • Allows you to hold the remaining shares for long-term capital gains.
        • The shares you elect to hold may subject you to AMT but will be eligible for capital gains treatment if you hold them for 1 year and 1 day from the date of exercise.
3. Exercise and hold.
    • You exercise your options and hold 100 percent of your shares for future appreciation (or loss).
    • Requires you to come up with cash for meeting all the "costs" of exercising (i.e., pay the strike price, pay the taxes, pay the brokerage fees).
    • What effectively happens in an 83(b) election (you pay to own the shares, incur the total tax liability, and hold the actual stock, not the option, until the vesting period and/or restrictions expire).
4. Reverse dollar-cost averaging (systematic exercise program).
    • Commonly used as part of an overall strategy to "unwind" a concentrated position resulting from stock option compensation.
    • Methodical approach to exercising a specific number of options at a specific price as a means of
        • Diversifying an investment portfolio by taking the cash proceeds and investing in other investments.

- Providing tax-efficiency by straddling different tax years and balancing the investment gain with the corresponding increase in taxes.
- Managing the expiration dates with market conditions and your desire to keep more of what you've earned.

Knowing the mechanics of paying for your options is important, but the critical factor in your equity compensation strategy is knowing *when* you should exercise your options. This is a particularly challenging area in terms of developing a strategy and establishing the corresponding decision-making criteria because it should be driven by your individual financial objectives and circumstances. There is no "one size fits all" approach to managing stock option compensation.

There are, however, some general principles you can use as guidelines for developing an approach to managing your equity compensation. These principles are related to the types of stock options you are awarded and provide you with a starting point in terms of developing a framework within which to view your situation and begin to determine a strategy that makes sense for your unique circumstances.

Nonqualified Stock Options

Because NQSOs are taxed as if your employer gave you a cash bonus check (the spread between the strike price and the market price on the day of exercise is subject to payroll and ordinary income taxes), you should think of this form of equity compensation as a complicated way to receive cash.

The most common strategy for NQSOs is to execute a same-day sale (exercise and sell), take the cash proceeds, and use the money for whatever financial goal is appropriate at the time: whether that be paying down or eliminating debt, funding your children's education expenses, diversifying your investment portfolio, paying life insurance premiums, or putting a down payment on a house.

A sell-to-cover strategy might be used for NQSOs if the employee intends to earmark a particular block of stock for future stock swaps and the employee has a pretty strong feeling that the stock price will continue to appreciate.

An exercise and hold strategy rarely makes sense for NQSOs as it would be much less complicated and much less costly (due to the payroll taxes and income taxes due upon exercise) to purchase those shares through an outside brokerage account if an employee were interested in the company strictly as an investment. This approach also perpetuates the problem of concentrating your wealth in a single company's stock.

One advantage of NQSOs is the opportunity to defer taxes and allow market price appreciation in the stock. By delaying the exercise of the option, the employee puts off paying payroll and ordinary income taxes until the stock price and the corresponding payout are higher. Paying attention to expiration dates and implementing a tax-savvy exercise schedule become important in these scenarios as the employee will want to establish market price targets for exercising specific grants and make every effort to level the tax liability over several years of an exercise strategy.

Incentive Stock Options

An ISO grant can be characterized as stock compensation instead of the cashlike compensation associated with NQSOs. The employer intends for the employee to buy stock in the corporation and hold it as an investment, sharing in the risks and rewards associated with owning that company's stock. As the recipient of this type of compensation, the employee has the prerogative to convert an ISO to an NQSO through a disqualifying disposition, effectively converting the grant from a stock award to a cashlike award.

The most common strategy for ISOs is the sell-to-cover approach. This minimizes the employee's actual out-of-pocket expense for taking ownership of the shares and starts the clock in terms of the holding period requirements (one year and a day after exercise and two years after the date of grant) to qualify for capital gains taxes. The spread between the strike price and the market price on the day of exercise is, however, an AMT preference item and may well subject the employee to the alternative minimum tax.

In a rising stock market, even with AMT, this is a strategy for ISOs because the capital gains tax rate is typic lower than the employee's ordinary income tax rate and there is the potential for using the AMT tax credit in subsequent years.

But market conditions at the start of the new millennium have reminded us that what goes up in the stock market can come down, and the consequences of that for ISO option holders can be particularly costly. Many optionees made the mistake of exercising their ISOs when the spread between the strike price and the market price was significant (creating a big AMT liability) and then watching their share prices plummet by the time April 15 rolled around, leaving them without the resources to pay the AMT tax due.

Exercising ISOs within the first quarter of the calendar year gives the employee the best opportunity for evaluating his or her alternatives during the year. Depending on the stock's performance, the employee can effect a disqualifying disposition (selling shares on or before December 31 of the calendar year of purchase) on some or all of the shares to limit or completely eliminate the AMT liability.

If a plan allows, employees can also make an 83(b) election for ISOs. This would be a disqualifying disposition, converting the tax liability to payroll and ordinary income, but it also would eliminate exposure to AMT and begin the capital gains clock. This is a savvy strategy for employees of start-up companies that are early in the business cycle and in which the upside potential for price appreciation is significant. This effectively allows employees to pay a minimal amount of ordinary income tax, completely avoid AMT, and expose themselves to what is now the lowest tax bracket available, long-term capital gains.

The drawback of this strategy is that it accelerates taxes, exposing the employee to the risks of an 83(b) election: company solvency, stock market fluctuation, employment throughout the vesting period, and so on. This is definitely a strategy worth considering, but it should be weighed carefully.

Restricted Stock

Restricted stock awards, a hybrid approach to equity compensation, are taxed like a cash bonus. As the vesting restrictions lapse, the employee is subject to payroll and ordinary income taxes on the spread between the grant price and the market price on the day the restrictions are lifted. The optionee simply decides whether to "cash out" completely (same-day sale) or sell to cover, meeting the tax liabilities and holding the company stock for future appreciation.

The real opportunity with restricted stock awards is the 83(b) election. Many optionees realize this too late and fail to file the election within 30 days of being granted the actual award. By filing an 83(b) election, the employee volunteers to accelerate the payment of taxes on 100 percent of the shares awarded even though they are not fully vested. In effect, the employee pays payroll and ordinary income taxes on the spread between the grant price and the market price of all shares but cannot actually take ownership of those shares until the vesting requirements have been met. Once those requirements are met, however, the optionee is subject to capital gains tax instead of payroll and ordinary income tax.

In some instances this can be a substantial difference.

An employee would choose this strategy if he or she had confidence in the continued appreciation of the company's stock price and felt that the potential tax savings outweighed the volatility of the stock's market price. This strategy is not recommended if there is any chance an employee will not be employed by the company at the end of the vesting schedule (leaving for a better job, subject to layoffs, etc.). The last thing optionees want to do is prepay taxes on something they will not be around to collect.

Again, these strategies are very basic but give you a place to begin thinking about your own circumstances. It is useful to know what employees receiving various types of options could be doing to maximize their equity compensation. As you meet with professionals to assess their proficiency in planning for clients with stock options, their recognition, comfort, and understanding of these practices will also help you determine their suitability as your advisers.

The Exercise of the Exercise

When you think of your least favorite things, paperwork is probably near the top of the list. Receiving stock options as part of your compensation package will add considerable administrative responsibility to the process of getting paid. There are several critical documents and processes associated with your stock options that you must grasp to master "the exercise of the exercise." Some of these processes are internal—meaning your employer dictates the administrative procedure—and some are external (i.e., establishing an account with a brokerage firm to exercise your options and execute the purchase and/or sale of your company stock).

Following are the basic documents associated with your equity compensation. Samples of each of these documents are included in the appendixes for review and comparison.

Grant Agreement and Vesting Schedule (Internal Document)

Your introduction to stock option compensation most likely will begin with a stock option award.

You will receive a grant agreement, a formal written notification that the board of directors (or the compensation committee that reports to the board) has authorized a specific grant of stock options in your name. This letter will indicate several important details about your equity compensation:

- The grant date and/or grant number
- The types of options you have been granted
- Nonqualified, restricted, or incentive stock options
- The number of shares for which you have been granted options
- The strike price for each option
- The vesting schedule for those option shares
- The expiration date associated with that particular grant

Keep this piece of paper in a safe place. Like the deed to your house or your car registration, it represents a legal contract regarding property that potentially could belong to you and your family.

Stock Option Plan Document (Internal Document)

All equity compensation plans are governed by a formal plan document. Many employers provide their employees with a summary of the plan and make the actual plan document available only upon request.

You definitely want to request a copy for you and your advisers to review because the plan document governs your equity compensation—period. There are IRS rules, there are SEC guidelines, and there are accepted practices in equity compensation. Unless things are spelled out in the plan document for your employer's plan, do not assume that anything applies to your stock option compensation.

The plan document will specifically address issues such as the following:

- Who is considered an employee
- How disability is defined
- What happens when an employee dies
- How a participant can pay for his or her options (cash, promissory note, stock swap, cashless exercise, etc.)
- Whether the compensation committee has discretion to change any of the provisions in the plan or the grant extended to you
- What happens to an option if it expires unexercised
- Your exercise rights upon termination (voluntary or involuntary)
- How the company will satisfy withholding tax obligations
- Who is eligible to participate in the plan
- The term of the plan
- The term of the option
- How things will be handled in the event of merger, acquisition, bankruptcy, and so on
- How the plan can be terminated or amended

The plan document is an important piece of your compensation puzzle. You should have the most up-to-date plan document to give to your team of advisers (financial planner, certified public account-ant, attorney) for their review and interpretation. Understanding the nuances of your company's particular plan could make a big difference in your ability to pocket more of your stock option com-pensation.

Exercise Notice (Internal Document)

Your company shares in the administrative burden of your stock option compensation. Because the type of option you are granted and how and when you choose to exercise that option affects your employer's accounting and payroll tax reporting requirements, your employer is required to keep detailed records of your option activity.

You will be asked to complete an exercise notice as part of actually exercising your options and taking ownership of the stock granted to you. Depending on the employer and its arrangement with various brokerage companies, you may have to provide the notice to the broker, who in turn will provide it to your company.

The point is that exercising your options is not instantaneous like calling your broker or trading over the Internet. While some com-panies have streamlined this process and moved it on-line, the vast majority of employers offering stock options to their employees still use the phone and fax to facilitate their equity compensation pro-grams.

Be prepared for the exercise process to take some paperwork and patience, especially the first time you do it.

83(b) Election Form (Internal and External Document)

The IRS has not created an "official" form for making this election, but many companies include a Section 83(b) election outline with their option agreements or exercise notices. If this form is not provided, you can create your own (see the Appendix for a sample), sign it and send one copy to your company, one copy to the IRS office where you send your annual income tax return, and attach one copy to your tax return in the year in which you make the election. Because use of the 83(b) election is "time-sensitive," it is recommended that you send the forms by registered mail so that you have a record of notification being received by the appropriate parties within the 30-day window required.

Brokerage Account Application (External Document)

Whether your employer uses a captive broker—a single brokerage firm to handle all employee stock option activity, allowing your employer to concentrate its record-keeping requirements with one company and publish exercise process procedures and materials that can serve all employees—or allows the use of multiple brokerage firms, you will want to establish a brokerage account before exercising your options. The actual application process probably can be completed on-line or over the phone.

It is very helpful to have this account established in advance so that in completing the necessary paperwork, you can reference the account number and the address and phone number of the broker and have a general idea of which department at that brokerage firm handles employee stock options (many firms have segregated these services because of their administrative intensity).

Margin Agreement (External Document)

If your plan document allows (or does not specifically prohibit) you to conduct a "cashless exercise," you will want to sign a margin agreement as part of establishing your brokerage account. This agreement supplements the new account application process (see Appendix) and involves the extension of credit by the broker to you, the account holder. That credit is secured by collateral in the account (the stock you are purchasing or have purchased), and the amount you borrow will be charged interest at the varying rates described in the agreement.

A nationally known law firm launched an investigation concerning allegations that brokers at a variety of prominent brokerage firms pressed their clients into investment strategies that recommended employees exercise their stock options and borrow against the value of their shares by placing the acquired shares in a margin account. These strategies did not involve investment diversification, nor was a full explanation of the risk involved given to the employees.

When the prices of these companies fell, the clients' shares were sold to meet "margin calls," leaving the employees with little or no cash and a significant and unexpected tax bill.

Source: *Internet Wire*,
December 3, 2001,
Klayman & Toskes, P.A.

If used correctly and only for the purposes of realizing your equity compensation, margin is an effective tool (we will discuss margin further in Chapter 8). If misused, margin accounts can result in significant investment losses and unanticipated tax bills. Just ask the chief executive officer (CEO) of a software company who had to sell $3 million worth of his company's stock at the market low to cover his margin call.

It is important that you "get ready to be ready" to exercise your stock options. Employees who make the mistake of leaving all the administrative aspects of exercising their equity compensation to the last minute create undue stress and anxiety for themselves; this is the financial equivalent of cramming for a final exam. Get as much of the paperwork associated with exercising your stock options out of the way so that you can focus on developing strategies for realizing your compensation and not get bogged down in last-minute administrative tasks that become urgent but are not the most important aspect of your stock option strategy.

Chapter Checklist

- Decide why you should exercise your options.
- Consider your alternatives in terms of when and how you might exercise your stock options.
- Reconcile your willingness to endure risk and volatility in determining whether you will cash out or exercise and hold.
- Understand the consequences of your various choices as they relate to your type of option compensation.
- Identify and create files for each type of document you will need to exercise and, immediately or eventually, sell your equity compensation:
  - Grant agreement with vesting schedule
  - Stock option plan document
  - Exercise notice
  - 83(b) election form
- Establish a brokerage account to facilitate the exercise process:
  - Margin agreement, if applicable

8

OP-TION-EER-ING®
(OP´SHE-NIR´ING)

n. 1. The art and science of effectively managing stock option compensation. 2. Maximizing the realized value of company stock options to achieve your individual financial objectives. 3. Efficient maneuvering around and painstaking management of the IRS tax code as it relates to equity compensation. This chapter introduces the Optioneering® process, a method of integrating a modified approach to comprehensive financial planning with the analytics required for maximizing equity compensation. The Optioneering® financial planning process specifically addresses the areas of cash management, net worth calculation, taxes, and estate planning, while the Optioneering® analytics system tackles the challenges of optimizing stock option compensation by modeling a variety of exercise strategies to achieve your financial goals and objectives.

Successful professionals are experienced in developing and implementing strategic plans. They have several critical measurement tools they work with every day (market share analysis, inventory reports, balance sheets, profit and loss statements, quarterly sales comparison reports, etc.) that give them insight into how their businesses are performing and allow them to make judgments about

129

where they are going and how best to get there. They use these tools to make decisions that affect capital spending and investment in future projects. These tools are instrumental in evaluating "what if" scenarios and looking at the consequences of changes in the marketplace, competition, and other planning assumptions. In essence, these tools provide the foundation for all decisions regarding the future of the business. These professionals are also very proficient in delegating specific responsibility to skilled individuals or teams in order to execute a plan as efficiently and effectively as possible and then managing the deliverables of that plan accordingly.

When it comes to managing their personal finances, however, most professionals find themselves without the proper tools to assess their circumstances. They are hard-pressed to project their net worth or tax liability from year to year. A personal cash flow analysis that compares year-to-year results is almost unheard of. In terms of effectively projecting retirement savings plan growth, the impact of inflation on spending, and potential estate tax liability, most wouldn't know where to begin.

These savvy decision makers also tend to misplace the principles of strategic planning and forget the value of employing experts or outside consultants in the design and implementation of a personal financial blueprint. Our culture has trained us to be good consumers of products and services, but we've been conditioned to make those purchase decisions in a vacuum. We fall into the trap of believing we can and should manage our financial concerns on our own and find ourselves at the mercy of the traditional sales process (Figure 8.1) as opposed to a professional advisory process (Figure 8.2).

How is it that we are good consumers of individual products and isolated services but don't understand how to benefit from a relationship with professional advisers? The answer is that our consumer culture is product and transaction driven, not process driven. Managing your stock option compensation and overall financial plan is a process, not an end result. It's an ongoing method of educating yourself about the choices available to you that is designed to provide you with a context within which to make good judgments and decisions. A process-driven mentality helps us understand that the fees we pay advisers are investments, not expenses.

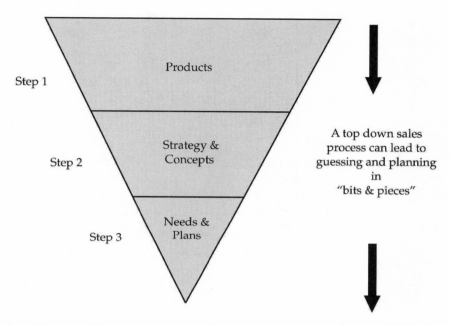

Figure 8.1 Traditional sales process. (*Source*: Private Advisory Group, LLC.)

The high-net-worth individuals of this world are masters of "the process." They've internalized the advisory paradigm and have become proficient at employing professionals to provide them with the tools and resources necessary for maximizing their return while minimizing their risk. The cliché "the rich get richer" exists because of this attitude, their willingness to assume the role of CEO for their financial well-being and pay for advice even on subjects about which they are already knowledgeable. That does not imply that every stock option recipient needs a high-priced entourage or will qualify for some of the programs that are available only to the wealthy, but it does suggest a need to reframe your thought process as it relates to managing your financial affairs.

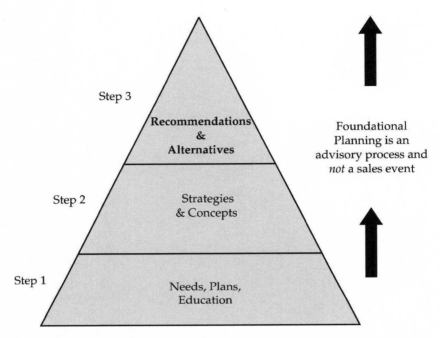

Figure 8.2 Professional advisory process. (*Source*: Private Advisory Group, LLC.)

The Optioneering® approach is holistic and provides anyone receiving stock options with a decision-making methodology designed to deliver insight into the consequences of multiple exercise strategies and allows a side-by-side comparison of predictable outcomes based on certain planning assumptions. Only by making these comparisons can stock option recipients make educated (and less emotional) decisions about the risks and rewards they are willing to encounter and endure. The results of Optioneering® analytics must then be integrated into a comprehensive financial planning process that has been modified to account for the complexities of equity compensation (see Figure 8.3). Optioneering® empowers an employee to exercise a stock option with a specific purpose in mind.

Let's look at some typical planning situations that demonstrate that we don't always know what kinds of questions we should ask to make a decision:

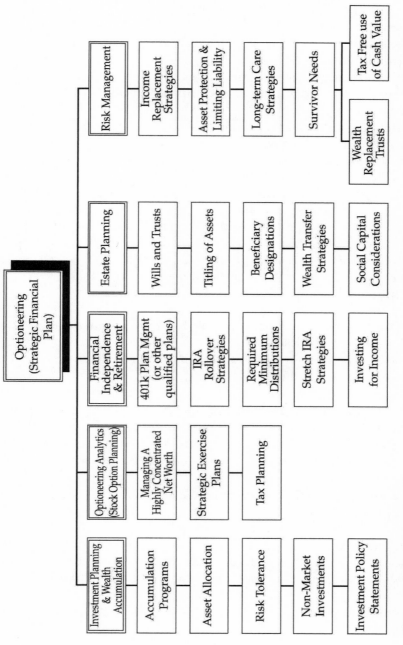

Figure 8.3 Optioneering®

- Buying a house or car leads to buying property and casualty insurance:
  - But how do you know how much is enough?
  - Should you have an umbrella policy?
  - Should you choose a higher deductible?
  - How do you compare one company's policy with another company's policy?
- Having a child drives the decision to purchase life insurance:
  - But how do you know which kind of policy or term of coverage is best suited for your circumstances?
  - Is the death benefit the only consideration?
  - How much life insurance does the family need if you aren't there to provide for them?
  - Coworkers have told us to buy term and invest the difference, but some good friends swear whole life is the only way to go. How do we know what's right for us?
- A relative or friend offers an investment tip on a stock:
  - But does it fit into your asset allocation strategy?
  - Do you even have one?
  - Do you have disciplined buy-sell criteria for managing your investment portfolios?
  - Do you actually know how your portfolio has performed over the last year? The last three years?

Now add stock options to the mix and try to determine when and if you should exercise options to create the liquidity for some of these concerns. How can you be expected to know the right questions to ask? That's the role of an experienced adviser using the Optioneering® approach to planning.

You want to work with professionals who will help you evaluate your needs in the context of a broader, strategic plan and then assist you in selecting the products or services that fulfill the needs you've identified as a priority. Importantly, you want these advisers to support you in the ongoing implementation of your entire plan, not earn their compensation only by selling you a single part of your plan.

Optioneering® is a concept that applies the basic principles of comprehensive financial planning to individuals with employee stock options. The subtle but important nuances associated with equity compensation make for significant considerations in the formal planning process.

> Comprehensive Financial Planning + Optioneering Analytics = Optioneering®

The Optioneering® Process

Any employee receiving stock option compensation should approach his or her personal financial planning as an Optioneering® initiative. Following is a broad outline of the components of the process, followed by some details that relate to the nuances of equity compensation and some examples of each component.

Optioneering® Steps

Take the following steps:

1. Decide what your goals are: what you're trying to accomplish in terms of time, money, and quality of life.
2. Identify and retain a financial quarterback—a personal chief financial officer (CFO)—and, with his or her help, a team of experienced, competent advisers.
3. With the team's guidance, develop a long-range strategy that further defines your needs, goals, and timelines.
4. Develop and agree to specific measurements for assessing your progress toward your objectives.
5. Complete Optioneering® analytics for integration into the overall plan.
6. Identify the predictable and potential obstacles standing in the way of your success.
7. Identify the methods and tools necessary for overcoming the roadblocks that have been identified in step 6.

8.   Create a written plan that provides you with a blueprint for
     your strategy and identifies the tactics to be used for achieving
     your goals.
9.   Identify the appropriate products and services for implementing
     your plan.
10. Hold your advisers accountable for the success of the plan.
     (Hold their feet to the fire on step 4).
11. Revisit your plan every 6 to 12 months (or if you experience
     any significant life cycle event, such as marriage, divorce, or
     birth of a child) and revise it accordingly.

Nuances of Equity Compensation

Optioneering® is a process that recognizes that employee stock option compensation is an ambiguous asset and that the recipients of
such compensation have unique planning considerations.

Specifically, stock option compensation places additional planning
emphasis on six key areas:

• Optioneering® analytics
• Cash management
• Net worth calculation
• Risk Management
• Taxes
• Estate planning

Optioneering® Analytics

The process within the process of Optioneering® manifests itself in
optimizing your equity compensation through a series of modeling
exercises that allows you to make educated decisions about the risks
and rewards associated with your stock options. The analysis is designed to create a decision methodology for you to navigate using
the following steps:

1.   Determine your planning assumptions.
     • Your annual income and tax bracket

- The anticipated market price appreciation of the company's stock
- The likelihood of future grants

2. Create a current inventory of stock option compensation, both vested and unvested.
   - Type(s) of option(s) awarded
   - Expiration dates
   - Vesting periods
   - Strike price for each grant

3. Establish your "worst case" and "best case" parameters by modeling two exercise strategies: cash out today and postpone exercise activity until expiration.
   - Worst case: cashless exercise in all vested options at current market price (likely scenario in the event of merger, acquisition, or termination)
   - Best case: cashless exercise assuming maximum holding period and constant stock price appreciation
   - All modeling integrates tax consequences and projects "take home value"

4. Model a "reverse dollar-cost-averaging" scenario.
   - A systematic exercise program that unwinds your option compensation over a period of time
   - Identify historic "high points" related to stock's trading range (in the instance of an IPO, use comparable company in industry sector)
   - Evaluate insider buy/sell activity to determine any discernable patterns
   - Identify targeted price points for exercising specific grants based on strike price, vesting period, and expiration date

5. Revise all scenarios based on changing your underlying assumptions in step #1.
   - Market price appreciation of the stock
   - Your income and tax bracket

6. Identify which conceptual strategy you are most comfortable with and begin modeling a variety of tax-efficient approaches to that model.

- Exercise all "in-the-money" options that are a specific dollar amount or a certain percent over the strike price
- Model the consequences of straddling tax years (partial exercise in December, partial exercise in January) as opposed to exercising all options in one tax year
- Balance the exercise of NQSOs with ISOs in an effort to minimize and eliminate AMT exposure by raising your ordinary income level through the NQSOs (or disqualifying some of the ISOs to achieve the same result)
7. Plug the "take home value" of your preferred scenario into the asset allocation, wealth accumulation, and net worth components of your comprehensive financial plan.
   - Evaluate impact on your investment diversification strategy, timing, and platform (Figure 8.4).
   - Determine impact on amount and timing of investments related to core, intermediate, and speculative investments (Figure 8.5).
8. Re-run your models at least twice a year.
   - As the market price changes, so will your projections for all these planning areas.
   - As events in your life change (e.g., marriage, birth of a child, divorce, disability), so will your needs in these planning areas.

Cash Management

Realizing the value of your stock option compensation requires cash in one form or another. It can be cash from your checking account, cash you borrow through a margin agreement at a brokerage firm, or cash you generate from current or future payroll checks from your employer.

The bottom line remains "it takes money to make money."

If you work for a pre-IPO company and elect to take ownership of your equity compensation prior to the company going public, you will have to come up with the money on your own—you cannot set up a margin agreement with a broker for a stock that isn't publicly traded.

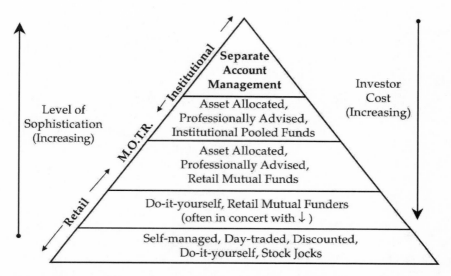

Figure 8.4 Service and cost, an inverse relationship. (*Source*: Don Parker, CFA)

And paying to exercise your shares is not your only concern. Being prepared to meet your tax obligation must be part of your cash management strategy, as we discussed in Chapter 6. Even if your employer withholds the appropriate payroll taxes, it may not withhold enough money for your ordinary income tax liability. You will want to accurately project your total tax obligation and prepare to meet it without subjecting those funds to market risk.

This lesson became painfully obvious to many unfortunate employees in 2000 and 2001 who exercised their options and counted on stock market appreciation of those shares for paying Uncle Sam. When the market values declined, these folks found themselves with a tax bill they could not meet by simply selling their shares in company stock. They had to look at other assets to provide the funds for paying those taxes—never a "first choice" from a planning perspective.

Traditional financial planning fundamentals recommend cash reserves of three to six months of living expenses. Employees receiving stock option compensation will have to project their cash needs in addition to that amount as a sensible place to start.

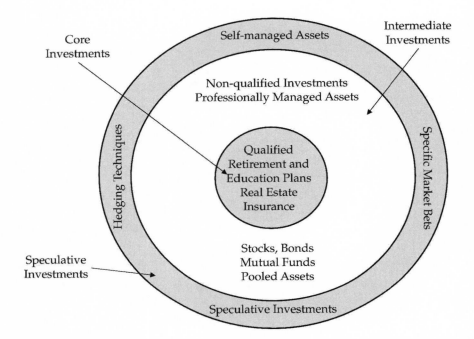

Figure 8.5 Investments: core, intermediate, and speculative. (*Source*: Don Parker, CFA)

Net Worth Calculation

Calculating an individual's net worth is fairly straightforward:

$$\text{Assets} - \text{Liabilities} = \text{Net Worth}$$

Many employees make the mistake of considering 100 percent of their stock option compensation as an asset and/or calculating the value of those options incorrectly.

The fact is, you can only consider vested options as true assets on your personal balance sheet. And you can only contribute the "take home" value of those vested options in the overall computation. Table 8.1 compares the common calculation with the correct calculation.

Senior executives and entry-level personnel make this mistake alike; stock option compensation is a confusing asset for any indi-

Table 8.1

	Common Calculation	Correct Calculation
# of options granted:	10,000	10,000
# of options vested:	N/A	2,000
Grant price:	N/A	$25.00
Market Price on date of Calculation:	$38.25	$38.25
Value of options for Net Worth calculation:	$382,500	$17,060*

*$38.25 (market price per share) – $25.00 (strike price per share) = $13.25 (exercise value per share);
$13.25 × 28% withholding for income taxes = $3.71; $13.25 × 7.65% for payroll taxes = $1.01
$13.25 (exercise value per share) – $4.72 (combined income and payroll taxes) = $8.53 (net value per share);
$8.53 (net value per share) x 2000 shares = $17,060 (take home amount)
The stated "take home" amount does not include the fees associated with brokerage commissions or margin agreements; actual "take home" value will be slightly lower.

vidual because the value of that compensation component is based on a fluctuating market price, a vesting schedule, and individual tax circumstances. You and/or your team of advisers can earn your keep by creating executive summary reports that provide you with an overview of your situation and delineate the areas of risk and fluctuation you will most likely encounter.

Risk Management

Managing risk and guaranteeing the protection of these assets usually involves buying some form of insurance. Employee stock options and the concentrated stock position they can create when an employee exercises those options and takes ownership of an equity asset in the form of company stock is no different. When a significant number of stock options are exercised and held—perhaps due to tax consequences or regulatory restrictions—a concentrated equity position is created that puts the paper wealth associated with that stock at risk of market price decline. There are a variety of risk management strategies that can be considered as a hedge against the market volatility of equity investments. These strategies employ contractual agreements between the employee (the investor) and an institutional partner and typically require that the investor meet a minimum net worth threshold.

The four most common risk management strategies for dealing with a concentrated stock position are purchasing a put option, selling a covered call option, creating a zero-premium (or cashless) collar, and a pre-paid forward sale.

Purchasing a Put Option. A put option provides downsize price protection. This strategy is for employees who have exercised their stock options, own the stock, and are concerned about a decline in the value of their concentrated equity position. The employee protects his or her investment by purchasing insurance against the possible decline in market value of the individual stock. Like car insurance and homeowner's insurance, the premiums are paid with the hope of never having to collect on the policy. If the stock price does not drop below the put strike price before the expiration date of the contract, the investor is out the cost of the premium paid to insure the value of their company stock—pennies on the dollar in comparison to replacing the value of the whole portfolio.

Selling a Covered Call Option. The sale of a covered call option provides current income to the investor and may allow limited participation in the stock price gains associated with the concentrated equity position. This strategy is appropriate for the employee who has exercised their stock options, owns the company stock, doesn't want to sell the stock at the current market price but does want to realize an income benefit from owning that stock. Basically, the investor trades unlimited upside potential on their stock for a specific amount of money they receive in the form of a premium payment. The employee contracts to receive a premium payment in exchange for guaranteeing that an interested buyer has the option to call or take ownership of the stock position at a pre-determined, higher price before the expiration of the contract. The employee will participate in all the price appreciation of the stock up to the call strike price. The employee's risk in using covered call options is the forfeiture of any gain above the contracted strike price. If an employee thinks a stock will trade in a fairly predictable range for a period of time but is not inclined to sell his or her company stock due to restrictions or the potential tax consequences of selling the stock, this provides an alternative method for creating liquidity with assets that may otherwise seem frozen.

Zero-Premium Collar.   Combining a put option with a covered call option in a single contract creates a zero-premium collar. This strategy works for an employee who has exercised his or her employee stock options, owns the stock, is concerned about the decline in value of their concentrated equity position but cannot or is not willing to pay the out-of-pocket expenses associated with a put option contract (in layman's terms, isn't willing to pay the cost of insurance). The employee trades some of the upside potential in the stock price for protection against the downside by using the premium received for an out-of-the-money covered call (meaning the strike price is above the current market price) to offset the cost of buying an out-of-the-money put option (meaning the strike price is below the current market price). In effect, both a floor price and a ceiling price are established for the stock position, hence the term "collar." The zero-premium or cashless nature of the transaction results from trading a premium received for a premium paid. The collar contract can be structured to last from months to years, ideally with both options (the put and the call) maturing simultaneously.

Pre-Paid Forward Sale.   A pre-paid forward sale is similar to a zero-premium collar in that it combines a put option with a covered call option; this approach is different in that the employee purchases a put option at-the-money (100 percent of the current market price) and sells an out-of-the-money call option (e.g., 125 percent of the current price). This strategy is suitable for employees who have exercised their employee stock options, own the stock, but are legally restricted or have another limitation on selling their stock. In exchange for this contractual collar, the employee will receive 75 per-

cent to 95 percent of the value of their stock and have no other obligations to the contracted buyer until the contract matures. The pre-
paid forward sale is similar to a home equity loan in that the employee collateralizes the concentrated stock position to receive a lump
sum of cash for their use. The employee's risk in this scenario includes the loss of the premium paid for the put, the forfeiture of
gains above the call strike price, and the loss of the concentrated
stock portfolio.

All of these risk management strategies involve binding agreements
with expiration dates. Like securing a mortgage or home-equity line
of credit, there are a variety of fees, commissions, and taxes that
factor into the pricing of these programs. Not every employee who
receives stock options will qualify for these programs, nor are these
strategies necessarily appropriate for every equity compensation
situation. Nonetheless, it is vital that employees receiving complicated compensation are aware of the sophisticated tools available for
maximizing those hard-earned rewards.

Taxes

Understanding the various taxes to which you are exposed and recognizing which taxes come into play based on the type of stock
option compensation you are awarded is important; this knowledge
makes you a better CEO of your finances and a better consumer of
professional advisory services.

But optimizing your exercise and sell strategy, projecting the
consequences of hundreds of different planning scenarios, evaluating
a variety of software programs designed to assist you with those
calculations…if you are a "hands on", detail-oriented type that enjoys
this type of analysis and have the time to devote to it, you will serve
yourself well by wading through the numbers; if that's not how you
want to spend your spare time or if you don't relish the thought of
mastering another new skill set, let your CFO and team of advisers
do the number crunching and come back to you with several viable
strategies for your consideration.

You want to know what time it is, not necessarily how the watch actually works.

Spend your time and money choosing your advisers and/or planning tools, not trying to create, for example, a spreadsheet for calculating your tax consequences. You need to know what the tax consequences are but that doesn't make you the best candidate for anticipating all the details and completing those computations.

Estate Planning

When you receive your first stock option grant, you need some estate planning. As discussed in Chapter 5, estate planning is simply making sure your assets are protected from creditors and predators and available to you during your lifetime...and then giving what you want to whom you want the way you want while saving every last tax dollar, attorney fee, and court cost possible. Many people make the mistake of thinking effective estate planning is a legal process; in fact, it's an economic process. The legal aspects of estate planning are important, but legal documents are only one of the many components of the tactical implementation of a strategic, financially based, estate plan.

Part of your role as CEO is to prepare your financial house to operate successfully without you. That means in the event of disability, death, divorce, loss of employment, etc., all predictable contingencies have been anticipated and the necessary safety nets are in place.

You may require trust documents, the re-titling of assets, durable or special powers of attorney, charitable gifting strategies, a wealth-replacement trust, the naming of successor trustees, a variety of asset protection plans...your plan will depend entirely upon your needs and your goals. Again, this is an area of specialty and expertise. Don't think that downloading a boilerplate template for a will or a trust and filling in the blanks gets the job done—you may spend more money undoing the damage you've caused yourself than if you had let professionals do their job to begin with.

Implementing Optioneering® Steps

Take the following steps:

1. Decide on your goals. Spend some time evaluating what's important to you. Many professionals resemble a hamster on a wheel, spending lots of time and energy but not making any progress. They simply don't take the time to determine when "enough is enough." You owe it to yourself to take a "time out" and determine your priorities.
2. Identify and retain a financial quarterback. Ideally, a fee-for-service financial planner fills this role. You can play this role yourself, but the question is "how well"? There are people who spend 100 percent of their working life learning and practicing in this area. We will discuss identifying the right professional for this job and the other members of your advisory team in the next chapter.
3. With the team's guidance, develop a long-range strategy that defines your needs, goals, and timelines. In this step, you will articulate specific goals regarding wealth accumulation (e.g., to have $1 million dollars in investment assets by a certain age), timing of financial independence (e.g., to "retire" from work as you know it by age 55), diversifying your current concentration in company stock (e.g., transition from 50 percent of your net worth in company stock to 10 percent over a 24-month period of time), and/or other priorities you identify during the process.
4. Develop and agree to specific measurements for assessing your progress toward your objectives. You will create meaningful "yardsticks" that allow you as your own CEO to hold your team accountable. Examples might include: increase your net worth by 10 percent per year for the next five years; earn an 8 percent after-tax return on all investment assets; reduce your annual tax liability by 20 percent; improve discretionary income by $1,000 per month through budgeting and debt elimination; eliminate current estate tax liability through formal gifting and the use of a wealth replacement trust.

5. Complete Optioneering® Analytics for integration into the overall plan. Identify the exercise strategy that most suits your financial goals and timelines, implement the most tax-efficient approach, and integrate the results with the other components of your formal financial plan.

6. Identify the predictable and potential obstacles standing in the way of your success. Play out multiple "what if" scenarios in the areas of disability, death, divorce, long-term care for one or both of your parents, etc.

7. Identify the methods and tools necessary for overcoming the roadblocks that have been identified in step #6. Determine what strategies may be available through your benefits program at work (e.g., group disability or long-term care insurance), any appropriate contingency planning that can be put in place, and what problem-solving approaches prove most cost-effective in addressing the issues identified.

8. Create a written plan that provides you with a "blueprint" for your strategy and identifies the tactics to be used for achieving your goals. The plan should include an executive summary that provides specific observations and recommendations.

9. Identify the appropriate products and services for implementing your plan. Due diligence related to products and services should result in a comparison of recommendations, the associated costs, and a cost/benefit analysis of each recommendation.

10. Hold your advisers accountable for the success of your plan. Conduct quarterly, semi-annual, or annual reviews based on the measurement criteria agreed upon in step #4.

11. Revisit your plan every six to twelve months (or if you experience any significant life cycle event—marriage, divorce, birth of a child, etc.) and revise it accordingly. Get into the habit of revising this plan on a consistent basis. The more you revisit the plan itself, the better it will serve as a roadmap for you and your team.

Revolutionary? No. Difficult or complicated? Not really. But like dieting or exercise, the payoff comes with consistency and discipline over the long haul.

A financial plan is not something you get after you've filled out a questionnaire or met a few times with an adviser; financial planning is a philosophy or state of mind that allows you to make educated decisions about financial concerns throughout your lifetime. It's a commitment—mentally, emotionally, and financially—to being the president or CEO of your financial well-being and surrounding yourself with the most capable board of advisers and planning tools you can muster. Like any successful endeavor, it will require time, effort, and continuous education. You will have to accept the fact that this is not a "do-it-yourself" project anymore—meaning you owe it to yourself and your loved ones to benefit from the power of many minds tackling the challenges posed by your unique circumstances, goals, and timelines. You can be as involved or as hands off as is comfortable for you but the fact is you've reached a point where doing what you've done up to this point in time is no longer prudent. You've graduated to the big leagues and need to staff accordingly (more on that issue in the next chapter).

Optioneering® is an extremely rewarding process if it is executed correctly. The key to success is choosing an advisory team and/or appropriate tools that are well suited to you. And selecting that team or those tools can be like dating—you will have to kiss a few frogs before meeting that perfect match.

But don't despair!

The time you invest in identifying your financial quarterback and his or her supporting cast, as well as the tools and yardsticks you will use to manage your wealth and become a better steward of your finances will be the best investment you can ever make. Some of you will insist on being both CEO and CFO—so be it. Some people believe that no one else will ever care about their finances more than they do and are most comfortable micro-managing the process; it can work.

But the wealthiest people on this planet—savvy individuals when it comes to money—choose advisers who educate them about the alternatives so they can make their own decisions. You should never relinquish control or decision-making as it relates to your financial well being, but that doesn't mean you can't employ people to do the legwork, be responsible for providing you with the analysis, or complete the due-diligence in terms of products and services available in the marketplace.

Optioneering® is a paradigm shift…away from transactions and toward process. You want to put yourself in a position of paying for expertise and advice, not a product or service. Implementing a plan that you decide is appropriate will result in the need for products and services…but those decisions come after the hardest work—creating the strategic blueprint—has been completed. You should seek every advantage available to you in determining what formal plan is appropriate for you and those important to you. Read on to learn how to recruit a team that can move you to the next level.

Chapter Checklist

- Recognize that Optioneering® is a process within a process
  - Comprehensive financial planning
  - Optioneering® analytics
  - Holistic approach
- Strive toward an advisory process that educates you.
- Focus on the six key planning areas related to stock option compensation:
  - Optioneering® analytics
  - Cash management
  - Net worth calculation
  - Risk management
  - Taxes
  - Estate planning
- Make the paradigm shift toward process and away from transactions.

9

RECRUITING YOUR
TEAM OF ADVISERS

This chapter provides a framework for identify-
ing, interviewing, and selecting professional
advisers. It also outlines methods for optimizing
the use of that professional team.

Recruiting your personal board of advisers is a serious matter that
"just sort of happens" for most people. You ask a few people who
does their taxes or investments or a friend mentions that he recently
had a will drawn up and cites an attorney's name in passing. Because
we tend to view our relationship with these advisers as limited and
isolated, involving one-time or once-a-year events, we don't give it
much thought or conduct the necessary due diligence.

That attitude has to change.

It's time to adopt an Optioneering® mind-set that makes you the
CEO of your financial well-being and challenges you to surround
yourself with a personal CFO and a board of advisers hand picked
through a structured selection process for their competence, compat-
ibility, and commitment to your long-term success. This is a group
of experts who are philosophically aligned with you, work well with
other professionals, and practice professionally in an advisory capacity, not a sales capacity.

This approach will require you to make an up-front investment of time and money. If done well, it will be worth every hour and dollar you invest in the process.

First and foremost, you want to work with fee-for-service advisers. You do not want to be dealing with individuals who have to sell you something to make money. You want to pay for time, talent, and objectivity, not be sold the product du jour.

Next, recognize that no single professional can do it all and do it well. You will occasionally come across an attorney who is also a certified public accountant (CPA) and/or licensed insurance agent or a CPA who also sells investments and manages money for clients. You are looking for professionals who have clarity of focus and insist on practicing within a licensed area of expertise.

Finally, you will want—at a minimum—to include a financial planner, an attorney, and a CPA on your team. These will be the disciplines and the areas of professional expertise that will be required to develop, execute, monitor, and maintain your personal plan. In some instances it may be appropriate to include a stockbroker or investment adviser, an insurance agent, a professional coach, or another individual whose wisdom and judgment you deem important in the overall makeup of your team.

Financial Planners

Your financial quarterback—your personal CFO—should be a fee-for-service financial planner with several years of experience and a few letters after his or her name (ChFC, CLU, CFP, CRPC, MBA, CFA, etc.). The professional designation is simply an indication of that person's commitment to continuing education—nothing more, nothing less. This individual, or in some instances, group should charge a healthy fee for the formal planning process (depending on where you live, those fees will range from $2,500 to $10,000 for basic planning; more complex planning, as will be the case with stock options, will go up from there).

Beware financial planners who do your planning for free; they will have to sell you something as part of the planning process to make any money, and so their objectivity is sacrificed from the outset. If the right thing for you to do is nothing, you want to pay an experienced, competent, objective professional to look you in the eye and tell you that's the case.

The reason your personal CFO should be a financial professional as opposed to a legal or tax professional is that the overall complexity of your circumstances and the appropriate strategies that come into play are best identified from a long-term financial perspective. You want someone who is comfortable running a lifetime cash flow analysis adjusted for inflation and taxes, someone who has expertise in prioritizing asset liquidation for tax efficiency, a professional who can illustrate the consequences of employing certain products or strategies in comparison to others, an expert in projecting estate tax consequences resulting from recent tax legislation, and someone concerned first and foremost with your ability to meet your overall financial goals.

Legal and tax professionals are absolutely critical in the tactical execution of your financial plan and add depth and dimension to the development of your overall strategy. However, they rarely have the tools and/or experience for projecting your net worth in 5- or 10-year increments based on a changing menu of planning assumptions, comparing your results year to year against benchmarks and established targets, or illustrating the cash flow and tax consequences of multiple exercise scenarios.

In other words, it is not the best use of an attorney's or an accountant's professional expertise or billable time to do personal financial modeling and reporting. That's the job of the financial professional, your personal CFO.

So how do you go about finding candidates for the position and selecting your personal CFO?

- Identify potential candidates:
  - Personal referrals: Ask friends, professional peers, or even your bosses if they are working with a fee-for-service financial planner they would recommend.
  - Professional referrals: Ask an accountant, a doctor, a lawyer, a dentist, or a business owner if he or she is working with a good fee-for-service financial planner.

- Professional associations: Contact your local financial planning association for a list of fee-for-service financial planners in your community.
- Nonprofit boards: If anyone you know is on a board of advisers for a community organization, ask that person if he or she works with any financial planners on the board.
- Conduct a personal interview:
  - Schedule a meeting with *all* the fee-for-service financial planners you've identified as potential candidates.
  - Your first consultation should be free of charge, and you should be prepared to learn the following:
    - Educational background, credentials, and professional associations.
    - Areas of experience and expertise.
    - A profile of the clients they work with.
    - The scope of their planning capacity, financial products, and related services.
    - Their infrastructure (local support, staff head count, accessibility, resources, "bench strength," etc.).
    - How they define financial planning and what you can expect to receive from them as a result of the process.
    - How they are compensated.
    - How much they estimate it would cost you to work with them; the first year and the annual renewal fees.
    - If they are in the habit of working with other professionals (CPAs, attorneys, stockbrokers, etc.).
  - Whether you like their style and have good chemistry during your meeting; this is an important position, and you want to work with someone you can trust, whom you have confidence in, someone you can disclose confidential information to without reservations, someone you plan to have a relationship with for many, many years.
- Ask for specific planning examples related to stock options:
  - You want to feel confident that the financial planner knows the difference between NQSOs, ISOs, and restricted stock awards.
  - You want to know that this adviser has command of the various tax consequences associated with different exercise strategies

and will not be learning about equity compensation on your nickel.

- You must be reassured this is not a one-time planning process and that the financial planner recognizes the need to monitor your company's stock price and your vesting schedule a minimum of twice a year.
- You want to know that you will benefit because the adviser has completed plans for employees of several different companies and has worked through a variety of planning scenarios.

Identifying and recruiting the right person (or persons) as your personal CFO will make it much easier to find an attorney and CPA for your advisory team. Any financial planner with experience in stock option planning will have a network of estate planning attorneys and CPAs he or she has worked with on behalf of other clients. Your CFO should volunteer to introduce you to the other advisers and encourage you to go through the same kind of discovery process with them. Simply remove the reference to *financial* and insert the word *legal* or *tax* in all the areas you discuss with the corresponding professional.

Above all, take your time to find the right team for you. You've waited this long to do formal planning; take the time necessary to do it right once you've committed to it.

Attorneys

You will want to work with attorneys who focus only on estate planning, are well versed in the complexities of the most recent tax law changes, and are willing to entertain several different "what if" scenarios from a legal perspective. The attorney you select should not have a preconceived notion of what you need before he or she knows your circumstances. The attorney should be interested in understanding your situation before proposing a solution.

Because you are a stock option recipient, your legal documents will be detailed and require a certain level of sophistication and customization, meaning you will pay a higher price for their preparation.

Again, we need an attitude adjustment, a paradigm shift. You're not "buying" a document; you're participating in an advisory process. View this is an investment, not an expense. You have to evaluate your return on investment, not your initial cash outlay. You want to know that if something happens to you, all the predictable contingencies are planned for, all the necessary safety nets are in place, and all the legal documents reflect your plan design.

CPAs

Most accountants, by their very nature, are historians. They are very good at looking at your circumstances through the rearview mirror and recording the appropriate financial history in all the right boxes. They tend to be very compliance-oriented, an occupational hazard that keeps them thinking "inside the box."

You want to find a CPA who is a strategist. They are out there, and they're worth their weight in gold. You want to make sure they have experience with AMT resulting from the exercise of ISOs and effective use of the AMT credit and are willing to work with your attorney and financial planner. And you want to manage your relationship with your CPA very proactively by paying attention to when you schedule time on his or her calendar. You simply will not get your money's worth from February through April with a CPA. The CPA and his or her team of resources tend to be buried with annual tax return preparation. Ideally, you would meet with your CPA and other advisers in June and late November or early December.

Once you've selected your team, you need to put its members to work. That also means they will put you to work. You will be asked to provide information regarding your assets, your debts, your spending patterns, your hopes and fears and aspirations—it's your past, present, and future being professionally managed for the first time. And everything will change as you go through different cycles in life. This is a constantly evolving process that can make the difference between knowing where you're going in your life and just letting things happen.

In putting your team to work, it's important to set the tone and manage expectations on an individual and a collective basis. Begin with your CFO and develop your "master plan." From there you and your financial quarterback should create an agenda for a team meeting. You will partner with your CFO in this part of the process because you will want to rely on that person's guidance on the sequence and topics to cover in that initial team meeting. You want to focus on the overall plan strategy so that the entire team grasps the scope and direction of your plan and then move into the tactical aspects of implementing that plan, identifying who does what, when, and where.

The purpose of the first team meeting is for you to articulate the role you want each professional to play in your planning process and assign specific responsibilities for each individual adviser. This will facilitate a sense of the team and allow the professionals to understand your perspective on each of their roles. Most of your meetings from that point forward will be held on an individual basis, but you want to create an atmosphere that encourages them to pick up the phone and contact another team member if a question or concern arises.

This approach should also reduce unnecessary fees associated with misunderstandings and confusion. Too often, the left hand doesn't know what the right hand is doing (because the client never introduced the advisers to each other, reviewed the overall strategic plan, and articulated the roles and responsibilities), and the result is time spent undoing what shouldn't have been executed in the first place.

You also want to review the payment structure associated with each adviser's services, as these structures can be quite different. Make sure you understand which initiatives are handled under a flat fee structure and which services will be billed hourly. Table 9.1 provides an overview of fees. Please understand that fees can vary dramatically, depending on which area of the country you live in, the complexity of your circumstances, the experience and expertise of your adviser, and your ability to work efficiently with your team.

Do not be afraid to negotiate up-front, challenge an invoice, or

Table 9.1. Fee-Based Adviser Fees

Adviser	Hourly Rate	Flat Fee Work	Other Fees
Attorney	$175/hr. – $350/hr.	Trust documents $1500 to $5000 ea.	Insurance commissions vary; paid by insurance carrier
CPA	$125/hr. – $225/hr.	Tax returns $100 to $500 ea.	Asset management 1.5% – 3.25% of investment portfolio Insurance commissions vary; paid by insurance carrier
Financial Adviser	$175/hr. – $300/hr.	Financial plan $2500 to $15,000 ea.	Asset management 1.5% – 2.5% of investment portfolio Insurance commissions vary; paid by insurance carrier

inquire about how you might receive a discount on services. Never forget that your advisers work for you and need to continually earn your trust and business or run the risk of being replaced.

Set the expectation that their meetings, phone conversations, and faxes to other professionals are not billable unless it's a meeting involving you or you are aware of the activity and know you will be billed for that time. Most professionals will welcome the opportunity to work with their planning counterparts and will understand the value of interacting with one another.

Remember that the vast majority of your advisers' clients don't operate this way either, so take advantage of the fact that most financial planners, CPAs, and attorneys would enjoy the opportunity to work together in a more strategic, team-oriented manner. If that doesn't appeal to them or you sense they are uncomfortable with that kind of arrangement, they are the wrong professionals for your team.

Finally, you should meet as a group at least once a year; you will also want to meet as a group if a significant change in your circumstances takes place (marriage, divorce, birth of a child, job change, etc.). Try to schedule that meeting during the fourth quarter of the calendar year. The purpose of the meeting should be to review your updated financial plan, provide each professional with an opportunity to present information to the group as it relates to your circumstances, discuss any significant changes you anticipate, raise any concerns or issues that need to be addressed, and make sure everyone is working in a coordinated fashion toward achieving your goals and timelines. Each adviser should leave that meeting with a "to do" list and have a specific date upon which he or she will respond to you.

As with most worthwhile endeavors, you will get out of this process what you put into it. If you're buying anything in the Optioneering® process, it's peace of mind. What's that worth to you and your family?

Chapter Checklist

- Develop your selection criteria for your advisory team.
- Identify potential candidates:
  - Fee-for-service versus commission-driven
  - Clearly articulated fee structure
- Conduct thorough interviews.
- Confirm experience and expertise regarding stock option planning.
- Develop the agenda for the first team meeting.
- Create performance measurement tools and success criteria for managing the team's performance.

10

THE OPTIONAIRE
NEXT DOOR

This chapter illustrates the real-world con-
sequences stock option compensation can have
for people on the receiving end. By examining
the mistakes made and the potential areas for
improvement, you will understand the need to
take this form of compensation seriously and
begin the formal planning process.

Perhaps the best way to demonstrate how stock option compensation
affects employees is to examine several real-world scenarios, analyze
the individual circumstances, explore the consequences of the actions
taken, and, with the benefit of hindsight, play Monday morning
quarterback and point out the things that could have been handled
differently for the benefit of the stock option recipient.

Following are actual cases that have taken place in the last few
years. The names of the employees and companies have been
changed to protect their privacy, but the details of their circumstances
closely resemble their actual experiences.

Case Study 1: A Little Bit Goes a Long Way

Employee profile: Scott Johnson, age 26, entry-level
                                     data processor.

Family profile:	Single.
Employer profile:	Large financial services company.
Employee objective:	Use proceeds of stock options to pay off student loan and credit card debt.
Stock options:	Single-year grant of 500 stock options (he's currently vested in 75 percent of his options) and opportunity to participate in a stock purchase plan via payroll deductions.
Type of options:	100 percent NQSOs.
Concentration:	Still has a negative net worth because of his debts.

Like many employees in their twenties, Scott is still trying to crawl out from the debt he incurred while going to school. He owes $6,000 in student loans and $3,300 in credit card debt and has an outstanding balance of $17,000 on his car loan. By the time he pays the rent, buys groceries, and makes minimum payments on everything he owes, Scott has just enough cash to join his buddies for a barley pop during happy hour. Although he realizes he's in the money on his options, Scott has heard from a number of people in his department that he should just put his stock option grant in a drawer and not worry about it for at least five years. As much as he'd like to take advantage of the discount available to him in the company stock purchase plan, he just can't swing the $50 per month that is required to participate.

20/20 Hindsight

Scott doesn't understand the true power of compound interest. If he exercised all his vested options, he would net approximately $4,400, enough to pay off his most expensive debt (the credit card debt) and pay down a little of the principal on his car loan. The reduction in Scott's monthly debt payment could then be split, with 50 percent going toward further debt reduction on the car loan and the student loan and 50 percent going toward the purchase of company stock through the discounted payroll deduction program.

While it's true that deferring taxes and hoping for stock price appreciation on nonqualified stock options can be a good strategy, it's not the right strategy for Scott in this phase of his financial life. He could be leveraging that part of his compensation to lay the foundation for future wealth accumulation.

Case Study 2: A Technology Company Goes Public

Employee profile:	Dan Watson, 37; software engineer, resident alien (green card status but not a U.S. citizen).
Family profile:	Married; spouse is Becky Watson, a U.S. citizen who works full-time as a consultant to an advertising agency.
Employer profile:	RSB, Inc., a Delaware corporation that provides e-business software solutions for logistics and distribution management.
Employee objective:	Use stock options as a wealth accumulation tool: maximize value and minimize taxes.
Stock options:	Several annual grants resulted in Dan being vested in 6,750 shares before the IPO in March 2000. Dan was scheduled to vest in another 3,917 shares during the summer of 2001 and 6,167 shares in 2002.
Type of options:	100 percent ISOs.
Concentration:	Dan's vested options represent 25 percent of the Watsons' total net worth.

Becky had received nonqualified stock options with a previous employer and had worked with a stockbroker to complete a cashless exercise several years before she and Dan met and married. Her only recollection of that experience was negative: She had been very disappointed with how her broker had handled the process and was quite shocked by how much money she didn't take home in the whole transaction. By her own admission, she didn't understand how stock options really work.

RSB, Inc., had been talking about going public for a year, and with the incredible success of other small technology companies going public in 1999, the Watsons were very optimistic about the potential windfall an IPO could bring. They had recently had dinner with a group of employees from another software company that had gone public at $12 a share, and now the company's stock was trading at $127 a share.

Dan and Becky bought and read the book *Consider Your Options* by Kaye Thomas and gave a copy of that book to their CPA. The local CPA said he found the book very helpful and further explained that it was in their best interest to exercise Dan's vested options before the company went public in an effort to minimize their AMT liability. In theory, the initial offering price (rumored to be around $14) would be the lowest price of the year, meaning that it would offer the lowest spread between Dan's exercise price of $2 and the market price on the day of exercise; that spread was a preference item for the AMT calculation.

Dan and Becky had never heard of AMT before, but they figured the CPA knew what he was talking about and took money out of their savings account to pay for exercising Dan's vested options in late February (6,750 vested shares at $2 = $13,500). In mid-March, RSB, Inc., announced it was delaying the IPO a few weeks because the underwriters were concerned about the timing of the offering. RSB did go public a bit later, but it was after the onset of the "tech wreck."

Dan and Becky were excited to watch the share price climb for a few weeks after the IPO, only to see it drop with the rest of the technology sector during the late summer and early fall of 2000. Because of the lockout period associated with the IPO (meaning that none of the employees who exercised their stock options could sell their stock for the first 180 days of trading), the Watsons could not have cashed out of their shares at a higher price right after the IPO anyway. Besides, they had exercised their options with the idea that they would hold out for the long-term capital gains status the

ISOs could provide; that was how their friends at other technology companies had made so much money.

Nonetheless, they were concerned about the AMT tax. By their calculation, they would be paying taxes on a spread that no longer existed; the market price had actually dropped well below the initial offering price. They went to talk to their CPA about it in early December, only to discover that when they had made the decision to exercise prior to the IPO—which they thought was a tax-savvy strategy—they had put themselves onto a 701 list, a restricted stock list that identifies the distribution of unregistered securities. Because the shares were actually issued before the company went public, they were not registered with the SEC. Unregistered shareholders are tracked on a list that is called the 701 list—jargon referring to the section of the law that governs the need for such a list—and must go through a time-consuming process to remove the restrictions from the stock certificates before they can receive the proceeds from the sale.

Because the shares were purchased before they were public or a registered security, those shares were now subject to more frequent and extensive blackout periods. Typically, that means that 30 days before a quarterly reporting period, the owners of restricted shares cannot trade them. In other words, the Watsons learned that they could not effect a disqualifying disposition (selling ISO shares within the same calendar year and in effect converting them to NQSOs for tax purposes) on any of the shares they had purchased in an effort to eliminate or minimize AMT because December was a blackout period for their restricted stock.

When the 2000 tax calculations were completed, the Watsons were subjected to AMT and paid an *incremental* $31,000 in taxes as a result (for a total tax bill of $56,000). Unfortunately, the share price of their company stock was so low (near the grant price of $2), they didn't have enough value in the stock to sell it and meet their tax obligation with the proceeds. And many of their other investments had dropped in value as well.

Like so many technology company employees that year, they made arrangements to pay the IRS in installments over the balance of the year 2001.

20/20 Hindsight

Although the damage has been done, we can learn from what happened to the Watsons. Small changes in their approach could have saved them thousands of dollars in taxes and penalties and interest.

Exercising ISOs before an IPO is still a viable strategy for minimizing AMT, provided that you are operating in a neutral or rising stock market. The key to making that plan work is recognizing that you will incur 701 status (unregistered stock that is restricted) and working within the confines of those restrictions, in other words, knowing that your window for effecting a disqualifying disposition is limited. In the case of the Watsons, they could have sold some of their shares in November (before the blackout period), converting a portion of their ISOs to NQSOs. This would have increased their ordinary income in tax year 2000 and eliminated or significantly reduced their AMT liability. They would have realized positive cash flow from the early exercise (perhaps earning back the cash they had laid out to exercise the options in the first place) and avoided being out of pocket on AMT taxes, late payment penalties, and the interest rate associated with the installment plan.

Another course of action for the Watsons would have been to wait and see. Instead of letting the fear of AMT drive their decision to exercise before the company went public, they could have simply waited for the public offering, let the lockout period expire, and kept an eye on market trends and company stock performance. When the market price dropped below the initial offering price and near Dan's strike price, they would have felt pretty good about doing nothing—with less cash out of pocket and no exposure to AMT.

The Watsons also could have used a home equity line of credit to pay the IRS instead of using the government installment plan. The interest incurred would have been lower and could have been used as a tax deduction in the next year. Dan and Becky have an investment diversification issue to contend with as well as some estate planning issues to resolve as a result of Dan's stock option compensation. They need to reduce their concentration in his company's stock and draw up the necessary legal documents to provide for

Becky's access to their stock option wealth in the event of Dan's disability or death.

Case Study 3: A Senior Executive Leaves His Company

Employee profile:	Mike Northrop, 44; senior executive, expatriate (U.S. citizen living abroad); recently resigned his position because he was passed over for promotion to president of the division he worked for in his company.
Family profile:	Married; spouse is Ling Lu Northrop, not a U.S. citizen; she is 41 and is not employed outside the home; they have one son in college.
Employer profile:	Multinational corporation selling pharmaceutical products.
Employee objective:	Use the proceeds from stock options to sustain their lifestyle until a new corporate position is secured and invest the balance as a retirement nest egg.
Stock options:	Nine years of annual grants had resulted in Mike being vested in over 70,000 shares of his former employer's stock. Mike had 90 days after his date of termination to exercise his vested options.
Type of options:	100 percent NQSOs.
Concentration:	Mike's vested options represent 90 percent of the Northrops' net worth.

As a successful corporate executive for over 15 years, Mike was accustomed to having his employer provide everything to support his family's lifestyle: income, housing allowances, medical and dental benefits, group life insurance, and assistance with federal income tax preparation and reporting. He was accustomed to having several people and entire departments available to assist him in the processing of paperwork and procedures, all those annoying little details that have to be addressed.

Mike did not have much experience exercising his equity compensation and had a fundamental belief that the company stock he was about to purchase would rise in market value at least another $8 to $10.

Mike waited until the eighty-seventh day of his 90-day window (late February) to exercise 69,610 of his in-the-money options. In executing this cashless exercise, Mike received a total of 14,802 shares after the company calculated his 28 percent withholding taxes (which was not his total tax liability of 39.6 percent), paid his broker transaction and margin loan fees, and paid the various strike prices.

Convinced the stock price would rise, Mike elected to keep 100 percent of his stock option exercise proceeds in his former employer's stock. One year later, after several withdrawals of dividend income to support his lifestyle while he looked for another executive position abroad, the stock price dropped 25 points and his total portfolio value declined about $322,000.

20/20 Hindsight

Mike had several planning strategies he could have employed if he'd only known about them and put them to work. First and foremost, because he resigned, he was in control of the timing of his termination from the company. Mike should have exercised 50 percent of his in-the-money options in December when he gave notice and then completed the balance of his exercise program in late February. This simple tactic would have allowed him to spread his total tax liability over two calendar years, minimizing the amount of tax he was exposed to in the highest bracket.

Second, in conducting his cashless exercise, Mike should have sold out of all but 10 percent of his former employer's stock and immediately diversified his investment portfolio. He had already realized 90 percent of the gain he had hoped to achieve and was in a position to reduce his investment risk significantly. As it is today, his future and that of his family hinge on the well-being of a single company for no compelling or logical reason other than his emotional attachment to the company's stock. Mike probably should ask the former employees of Enron or MCI or Tyco if they think it wise to keep all one's personal wealth and/or retirement savings in a single company's stock.

As in all stock option recipient cases, the Northrops also have some estate planning issues that need to be addressed, with particular attention being paid to the role of federal estate tax exemptions for non-U.S. citizens.

Case Study 4: "Underwater" Options

Employee profile:	John Peterson, 36; director of marketing.
Family profile:	Married; wife, Diane, does not work outside the home; two children, ages four and one.
Employer profile:	Multinational company manufacturing tools and household appliances.
Employee objective:	Use proceeds of stock options to supplement current savings toward college funding for the children and early retirement at age 58.
Stock options:	Four years of annual grants have resulted in John being vested in 1,425 shares of his employer's stock and on track to vest in another 2,475 shares by April 2005. John probably will continue to receive annual awards that will increase his total stock option inventory.
Type of options:	100 percent NQSOs.

Concentration:	Because the current market values of John's options are "underwater" (the market price of the stock is below the price at which the option was granted), the options do not contribute significantly to the Petersons' net worth at this time. If the stock price rebounds and approaches John's target price, however, his options will represent 36 percent of their net worth.

John assumed that there was no planning involved in managing his underwater options. He'd pretty much written them off as worthless and continued to focus on moving up the corporate ladder as a way to increase his income and contribute more to his family's financial goals.

He kept an eye on the company's stock price and looked at his grant agreements once a year as part of his financial spring cleaning but didn't really have a strategy in place for making decisions about his equity compensation.

20/20 Hindsight

Targeting specific exercise prices and determining which grants will be sold in which tax years is an ideal way to manage equity compensation awards, especially if they are currently underwater. John is in the enviable position of being able to play out several different "what if" scenarios without the pressure of having to make the decision right away. Importantly, the Petersons will know within a few dollars what they can expect to take home from each exercise after paying taxes and transaction fees.

With proper planning, John and Diane can set price targets for each grant, remain sensitive to expiration and vesting dates, and be as tax-efficient as possible by straddling tax years for the actual exercise activity. In addition, the Petersons should develop a specific game plan for the proceeds of each exercise activity (funding a 529 college savings plan for the children, supplementing their retirement investments, paying down credit card debt, financing the purchase of a new car, etc.).

John also can take advantage of this period of inactivity to "get ready to be ready" to exercise his options. Having never executed a stock option exercise before, he is totally unaware of what is involved in establishing a brokerage account and margin agreement with his company's captive broker and completing the notice of exercise paperwork required by his employer. He can get the paperwork out of the way, set exercise price targets for each grant, and communicate those targets to his broker so that his plan is on "autopilot" as much as possible. John and Diane also can identify specifically where the proceeds of each transaction will ultimately go.

In addition, John and Diane need to meet with an estate planning attorney to draft the required documents for appointing guardians for their children in the event of their untimely deaths, providing for the necessary decision-making capabilities in the event of disability for either one of them, and protecting their assets from the probate costs in a community property state.

Case Study 5: An Unexpected Death

Employee profile:	Georgia Hanson, 62; director of human resources.
Family profile:	Married; spouse is Gerald; Gerald is seven years older than Georgia and is retired from owning several restaurants. They have one daughter, Stacey, who is 34 years old.
Employer profile:	Multinational corporation selling pharmaceutical products.
Employee objective:	Allow the stock price to appreciate as long as possible before exercising to defer the taxes and increase the total value of the portfolio.

Stock options:	Eight years of annual grants (beginning when her company was acquired by a larger corporation) had resulted in Georgia being vested in over 30,000 shares of her employer's stock. Georgia had exercised a few thousand options in the previous year to pay for a cruise she and Gerald had wanted to take for several years.
Type of options:	50 percent Restricted Stock, 50 percent NQSOs.
Concentration:	Georgia's vested options represent 50 percent of the Hansons' total net worth.

Georgia Hanson loved her job and had adjusted to the corporate politics of the larger company that took over her employer in the early 1990s. She was especially pleased with the introduction of the stock option compensation program and was impressed with the wealth she had accumulated over the last couple of years. Georgia was planning to retire at age 65 and travel extensively with Gerald, who was being treated for prostate cancer.

Georgia died unexpectedly at work of a stroke.

Gerald and Stacey, after dealing with the funeral and burial arrangements, were left to make sense of Georgia's equity compensation and the role it played in settling her estate. Neither one of them knew much about the program or had personal experience with stock option compensation. After putting off the inevitable for several months, they turned to an attorney for assistance, and he informed them that they had lost all the stock options with Georgia's death.

Gerald didn't believe the attorney knew what he was talking about, and so he found a different attorney and called the company. The company explained that its plan had a provision that gave him, as the surviving spouse, one year from the date of death to exercise all of Georgia's vested NQSO options and that the vesting schedule on her restricted shares had been accelerated, meaning that they were now 100 percent vested.

Georgia had kept meticulous records, and so finding all the grant agreements and the corresponding vesting schedules was not difficult. Executing the exercise activity, however, was another matter.

Gerald's paperwork was just beginning. He would have to complete the notice of exercise paperwork necessary to inform Georgia's employer of any exercise activity. He also would have to change the titling of her brokerage account so that he would have the authority to give trading and cash distribution instructions to the broker. Gerald also had the responsibility for filing two tax returns: the final joint income tax return for him and Georgia and a return for the deceased estate. All this could be accomplished with death certificates and the appropriate court orders, but Gerald was having difficulty with his new attorney in terms of a sense of urgency and his health had deteriorated significantly since the death of his wife. Thus, Gerald found himself concerned with completing the proper planning for transferring his wealth to his daughter, Stacey.

To further complicate matters, Georgia had died one day before the vesting date on a rather large NQSO grant and Gerald did not know if the company would be flexible about it. His new attorney promised Gerald he would "look into the matter" for him.

20/20 Hindsight

When all was said and done, a significant amount of the Hansons' stock option wealth went to pay Uncle Sam and the attorney. The wealth erosion experienced by Gerald and, ultimately, Stacey could have been mitigated with proactive planning. Georgia's instinct to defer taxes as long as possible was not unreasonable, but it did result in some unintended consequences.

First of all, the restricted stock awards that Georgia earned could have, and in her circumstances should have, been handled differently. Within 30 days of receiving her restricted stock awards, Georgia should have filed an 83(b) election, choosing to pay taxes on 100 percent of the grant even though she was not fully vested. This would have changed the tax status of her restricted shares from ordinary income to capital gains and provided her heirs with a "step-up in basis" at her death. Because of her employer's successful performance in the stock market over the eight years she received these awards, this strategy would have saved her heirs tens of thousands of dollars in unnecessary taxes.

This strategy is not without its drawbacks, however, in terms of continued concentration in company stock. Ideally, the concentration perpetuated by the 83(b) election and the decision to hold the stock for capital gains would have been offset by the exercise and sale of NQSO options over the course of several years. Using the proceeds of these exercises, the Hansons should have diversified their investment portfolio every year. In a perfect world they would have set their price target for each grant, exercised when the market value hit that target, and repositioned the money in other sectors and industries or even in some nonmarket investments such as real estate.

Finally, the Hanson family accidentally implemented a "maximum tax and billable hours" strategy. Gerald ended up exercising 100 percent of the vested options as close to the anniversary of Georgia's death as possible (remember, he only had one year) not out of choice but out of necessity. The shock of her death, his failing health, and his lack of experience with options, combined with both attorneys' lack of expertise, led to unnecessary taxes and legal fees.

Unfortunately, neither Gerald nor his attorney (who did, by the way, bill him for "looking into it" but not resolving it) read the company's plan document. If they had done so, they would have uncovered the fact that a compensation committee appointed by the board of directors reviewed all circumstances for special exceptions in the case of disability and death. In all likelihood, given Georgia's tenure and good standing with the company, the committee would have made an exception regarding the timing of her death and the fact that the actual vesting date was one day later.

Case Study 6: Victim of Corporate Downsizing

Employee profile:	Marcus Holmes, 51; vice president of marketing for a large hotel chain; his department was eliminated in a corporate downsizing initiative in January 2002, and his termination date was seven days before his next vesting period.
Family profile:	Single but engaged to be married.
Employer profile:	Multinational company in the hospitality industry.
Employee objective:	Use proceeds of stock options to finance the starting up of a new business and supplement his retirement savings.
Stock options:	Ten years of annual grants and one corporate merger have resulted in Marcus being vested in 34,000 shares of his employer's stock in one plan and 32,500 shares in another plan.
Type of options:	100 percent NQSOs.
Concentration:	50 percent of Marcus's net worth is tied up in company stock.

Marcus had been with his company for 24 years and had a stellar reputation within the industry. Marcus had intended to retire with the company and had not exercised many of his options, thinking he would deal with them closer to his retirement in about nine years. He was caught off guard by the downsizing of his department and was scrambling to get things in order.

He spent several weeks negotiating his severance package and received the counsel of two attorneys as it related to the noncompete clause of the severance agreement and his stock option compensation. Both attorneys told him he had no flexibility in regard to his stock option compensation and would have to settle for the in-the-money options in which he was vested (the share prices were still quite depressed because of the lingering impact of the September 11, 2001, terrorist attacks on the travel and hospitality industry).

20/20 Hindsight

Upon review of Marcus's grant and vesting schedule, it became obvious that he would have been best served by employing a systematic "exercise and sell to diversify" strategy beginning in 1997. If he had instituted such a program, he would have had approximately $200,000 in investment assets sitting in a brokerage account, completely unrelated to his employment status. As it stands today, exercising his vested options that are in the money will result in about $65,000. The rest of his equity compensation is underwater and shows little promise of appreciating within the 90-day window afforded him by the termination.

Fortunately for Marcus, his stockbroker introduced him to a financial consultant who specialized in stock option planning. After her review of the plan document, she discovered that the compensation committee appointed by the board of directors of his former employer had complete discretion regarding the rules associated with Marcus's stock option compensation, and she believed he had some negotiating leverage as a result of being a long time, loyal employee caught in the unanticipated downturn in the market.

Marcus formally petitioned the board of directors, and they extended his exercise window beyond the traditional 90 days from the date of termination to the end of the calendar year. As a result of this extension, he will have the opportunity to see if any of his underwater options appreciate above the grant price and provide him with an opportunity to realize more of his equity income.

Case Study 7: A Bad Merger Ruins a Good Retirement

Employee profile:	Steve Winters, 61; regional sales manager for a drug distribution company.
Family profile:	Married with one daughter in medical school.
Employer profile:	Large corporation in the process of merging with a much smaller, innovative technology company.

Employee objective:	Use the proceeds of stock options and the stock purchase plan to fund retirement lifestyle and education expenses for his daughter.
Stock options:	Ten years of purchasing stock through a payroll deduction program had resulted in 3,000 shares; Steve also had been granted 1,150 stock options.
Type of options:	ESPPs and NQSOs.
Concentration:	Thirty-two percent of Steve's net worth is concentrated in company stock.

Steve retired from his company on March 15, 1999. At that time the company stock purchase plan and stock option exercise activity were frozen for 90 days because of the merger with the technology company. The stock hit a 52-week high in mid-April and then, in May, cratered to 35 percent of its value in 48 hours on the news that the acquired company had "cooked the books" to make the merger work.

Steve saw his company stock portfolio of almost $380,000 dwindle down to $140,000 in two days. Since that time Steve has exercised his options to pay for some outstanding medical bills for his wife and make tuition payments for his daughter. He estimates a real loss on his transactions of over $50,000, not in potential gain but in proceeds versus his actual investment.

20/20 Hindsight

Steve couldn't have known that the highly touted merger would turn out to be a sham. Obviously, the CEO, CFO, and board of directors had no idea they were being hoodwinked. Steve's big mistake was not diversifying or insuring his retirement nest egg well in advance of stepping away from the company. If he had purchased protective puts on the 3,000 shares he already owned through the payroll deduction program and exercised his options over the course of two or three years in anticipation of retiring, the bad news about the merger would have been an entertaining story to tell at cocktail parties instead of a financially devastating event.

Sophisticated Compensation Deserves Realistic Consideration

Stock options are not an academic form of compensation. They are awarded to employees who live in the real world and deal with practical, not theoretical, situations. These anecdotes are important because they illustrate some of the realities of equity compensation and bring to light the often unforeseen consequences that can accompany stock options. These case studies demonstrate that indeed, "the devil is in the details."

These are not isolated incidents. They are representative of the complexities and nuances associated with equity compensation. Stock options represent paper wealth—raw potential—that can be realized with proper planning. Ignorance and failure to plan, however, can result in unnecessary taxes, expenses, and erosion of wealth.

Do yourself a favor and begin the formal planning process. It's too expensive to ignore it any longer.

Chapter Checklist

- Recognize that the true value of formal planning lies in playing out the countless "what if" scenarios and addressing the issues that can arise before they happen.
- Understand that there is tremendous value in getting second and third opinions about the consequences of stock option compensation strategies.
- Appreciate that there are multiple solutions to the circumstances resulting from stock option compensation and that time and energy spent identifying those potential solutions will determine how much of your equity compensation you will realize.

Conclusion: Your Options with Your Options

The purpose of this conclusion is to reinforce the concept of investing time and money in the formal planning process. Stock option compensation creates a level of complexity that requires a paradigm shift in managing your personal finances.

Stock option compensation can be a fabulous wealth-building tool if you treat it as such. It is complicated and, unfortunately, is awarded to the unsuspecting. If it were up to me, every company that institutes an equity compensation program would be required to provide at least 12 hours of continuing education taught by experienced consultants and advisers from outside the corporation to its employees each year, dedicated to the various topics that influence the ultimate take-home value realized by each employee.

Your company has extended a potentially lucrative form of compensation; it's up to you to realize the full value of that reward. You are a successful professional and need to leverage the skills that have catapulted you into that enviable position for the benefit of your personal wealth. Having finished this book, you are more capable and better equipped to employ a comprehensive planning process designed to address the unique challenges of stock option compensation—the Optioneering® process—which could ultimately determine how much of your hard-earned equity compensation you realize.

Could you accomplish your personal financial goals on your own?

Undoubtedly, yes. But is that the best use of your time and talents?

Bright, ambitious, hard working people generally can accomplish any goal on which they set their sights. But the time you take to navigate the tax code; prepare the necessary income, cash flow, and tax projections; keep track of the legislative updates; master the financial planning software; run the necessary analysis with a menu of changing assumptions; complete the due diligence on suitable products and services; review the appropriate legal strategies; draft the necessary documents for an attorney to sign off on; implement the plan; and review it semiannually may be time you'd rather spend climbing the corporate ladder, watching your kids play soccer, pursuing your love of fly-fishing or meeting that "special someone."

You'll be limited to the scope of planning for your own circumstances. One of the benefits of working with experienced professionals is that they've worked on dozens of cases and can transfer that learning from one client circumstance to another. True, every brain surgeon has to start somewhere, but I'd prefer to work with a doctor—surrounded by an experienced anesthesiologist and excellent surgical nurses—who has completed the procedure several times before I lie down on the operating table.

I wrote this book out of frustration and a fundamental belief that as complicated as stock options can be, it is possible for anyone to have a better working knowledge of his or her equity compensation and learn how to maximize their potential wealth. My experience has led me to the belief that anyone who is serious about becoming a better steward of his or her finances will benefit from employing a team of experts; stock option compensation simply amplifies the need for professional expertise. Some may choose to do it on their own, and the Optioneering® process will help them in areas they may have overlooked.

Only you can decide what works best for you. My wish for you is that reading this book has brought some clarity to your understanding of stock option compensation and motivated you to play an active role in realizing more of what you've earned.

APPENDIXES

A GLOSSARY OF EQUITY COMPENSATION TERMS

adjusted gross income (AGI)   your total income from taxable sources minus adjustments such as contributions to your 401k account. Your AGI minus all other deductions (itemized or standard) and exemptions equals your taxable income.

alternative minimum tax (AMT)   a parallel tax calculation that may subject an employee exercising incentive stock options to taxes that otherwise would not be due.

blackout period   certain times of the year when company employees—typically insiders—are not allowed to sell their company stock or exercise their options. These periods, mandated by the SEC, coincide with the release of quarterly earnings information or circumstances related to acquisitions and mergers.

Black-Scholes option pricing model   a complex mathematical formula developed by Fisher Black and Myron Scholes, that is commonly used for valuing stock options. The equation takes into consideration the volatility of the underlying stock, the dividend rate, the current risk-free interest rate, the spread between the grant price and the fair market value of the stock, and the term of the option. This formula often is used in the division of marital assets in a divorce case.

capital gain   the increase in the value of a capital asset (anything of lasting value, such as stock acquired through the exercise of an employee stock option) that you realize when you sell the asset. If the asset was held for one year and one day after the purchase, the gain usually is taxed at a rate lower than the rate you pay on your salary.

capital loss   the amount you lose or give up when you sell a capital asset at a loss. You are limited to deducting up to $3,000 per year against your ordinary income tax (first deducted against capital gains, then against ordinary income) and carrying forward any balance exceeding that $3,000 into future tax years.

cashless exercise   also referred to as a "same-day sale"; the exercising of an option in which a broker lends the optionee the money to complete the transaction. The broker will then immediately sell 100 percent of the shares acquired in the exercise process, using a portion of the proceeds to cover the taxes, transaction fees, and margin loan fees and remitting the balance to the optionee in cash. Not all plans allow for this payment method.

cost basis   the actual cost required to buy stock in the company. In the instance of a stock option, this is equivalent to the exercise price. This cost is then compared to the amount received upon the sale of stock to determine the "spread" for purposes of calculating the applicable tax.

disqualifying disposition   occurs when an employee who has been awarded an incentive stock option elects to exercise and sell those shares before meeting the required holding periods (one year and one day from exercise and two years from the date of the grant). This essentially converts the incentive stock option to a nonqualified stock option for tax purposes.

83(b) election   a strategy that accelerates your tax liability before meeting the actual vesting requirements in an effort to convert future payroll and ordinary income tax into capital gains tax. Most commonly used with (but not limited to) restricted stock awards, this strategy must be executed within 30 days of receiving the stock through early exercise. An 83(b) election must be filed with the IRS and your employer.

employee stock purchase plan (ESPP)   an employee benefit plan defined by the IRS code, Section 423, that allows an employee to purchase company stock, often at a discount, through payroll deductions.

equity collar   a hedging strategy for option holders that sets a range around the possible stock price for your company's shares. This strategy limits both the upside and the downside of the stock price.

equity compensation   a method of paying employees and/or consultants, directors, and independent contractors with stock in the company as opposed to cash.

estate taxes   taxes levied by the federal and state government on the transfer of your assets after you die. These taxes are 100 percent voluntary and can be "zeroed out" with proper planning.

exercise   to take ownership of shares granted through an option. In the case of incentive, nonqualified, and ESPP plans, this requires a purchase. In the case of restricted stock, it requires meeting the terms of the vesting schedule.

exercise date   the date you take ownership of your shares by converting an option to a share of company stock.

exercise price   also referred to as the *grant price* or *strike price*; the price you pay when you exercise your option.

expiration date   the last date you are able to exercise your stock option; the option becomes worthless after this date.

fair market value   the amount a company's stock is worth on a given day and time; in terms of shares purchased through the exercise of a stock option, refers to the trading price on the appropriate exchange at the time of exercise.

incentive stock option (ISO)   a type of stock option that qualifies for preferential tax treatment provided that the optionee holds the stock one year and one day after exercise and two years after the date of grant, whichever is later. Under current tax law, the employee pays no taxes at exercise and will be subject to capital gains tax if the holding requirements are met. Exercise of ISOs may subject the employee to AMT. The company does *not* receive a tax deduction for this form of compensation.

income in respect of a decedent   a way to tax income earned before death that otherwise would have been included in the decedent's income if he or she had lived to collect it. This is a tax code mechanism that keeps certain assets from receiving a step-up in cost basis when assets are being transferred as a result of death, providing instead for a carryover basis that results in the beneficiary having to pay the income taxes that were never paid during the decedent's lifetime.

in-the-money option   occurs when the fair market value of the company's stock is higher than the exercise price at which the option is granted (as opposed to underwater and out-of-the-money options).

lockup period   a period after an IPO when some or all of the current shareholders are prohibited from selling their shares in company stock.

margin   the practice of borrowing money from a broker-age firm against the value of your brokerage account. Similar to a home equity loan; you collateralize a particular asset—in this case your stock—and leverage the underlying asset in an effort to create more buying power.

nonqualified stock option (NQSO)   a stock option that does not receive preferential tax treatment and is considered the equivalent of cash compensation. Optionees pay payroll and income taxes at the time of exercise and, if they hold on to the stock, are subject to capital gains treatment when the stock is sold. The company takes a tax deduction at the time of exercise on the spread between the grant price and the fair market value upon exercise.

option agreement   the contract between a company and its employee that sets forth the terms (strike price, number of shares, vesting schedule, expiration date of the option grant, etc.) of the option grant.

out-of-the-money option   occurs when the fair market value of the company's stock is lower than the exercise price at which the option is granted.

plan document   a legal, governing document that states the company's policies and procedures related to its equity compensation program.

restricted stock   (a) shares that are issued in a private placement and are not registered with the SEC. They cannot be sold unless certain requirements are met. These securities are also called Rule 144 stock or list 701 stock. (b) Stock that is granted by a company but is subject to specific vesting or performance requirements.

sell to cover   a method of exercising options through the use of a brokerage margin account, and then selling only enough shares to pay the taxes, transaction fee, and margin loan fee. This allows the optionee to hold the balance of the company's stock for future appreciation.

spread   the difference between the grant price of the stock option and the fair market value of the company's stock at the time of exercise.

stock option   the right, but not the obligation, to purchase a specific number of shares at a fixed price for a predetermined period of time.

stock swap   the practice of exercising stock options by paying for stock with previously owned shares of company stock instead of cash or cash equivalents (i.e., margin loan).

underwater option   occurs when the fair market value of a company's stock is lower than the grant price of the stock option.

unvested option   a stock option an optionee has been granted but does not yet have the right to exercise.

vested option   a stock option that can be exercised.

vesting   the process by which an option matures and can be exercised.

vesting period   the time period in which an optionee becomes eligible to exercise a specific number of options.

withholding   the taxes deducted from an employee's compensation by an employer. This is required when nonqualified stock options are exercised.

RESOURCES

Books

Better Than Money, David E. Grumpert, Lauson Publishing Company

The Complete Guide to Employee Stock Options, Frederick D. Lipman, Prima Publishing

Consider Your Options, Kaye A. Thomas, Fairmark Press

The Employee's Guide to Stock Options, Corey Rosen, National Center for Employee Ownership

Employee Stock Options, Gabriel Fenton, Joseph S. Stern III and Michael Gray, Stillman Publishing

Pay Me in Stock Options, C. E. Curtis, Wiley

Stock Options: An Authoritative Guide to Incentive and Nonqualified Stock Options, Robert R. Pastore, PCM Capital Publishing

Stock Options: Beyond the Basics, edited by Scott S. Rodrick, National Center for Employee Ownership

Stock Options for Dummies, Alan R. Simon, Hungry Minds, Inc.

Stock Options: Getting Your Share of the Action, Tom Taulli, Bloomberg Press

The Stock Options Book, 3rd ed., revised., edited by Scott S. Rodrick, National Center for Employee Ownership

Understanding Employee Stock Options, Rule 144 and Concentrated Stock Position Strategies, Travis L. Knapp and Nathan Reneau, Writers Club Press

Your Employee Stock Options, Alan B. Ungar and Mark T. Sakanashi, Harper Business

Websites[*]

www.fairmark.com

www.institutecdp.com

www.mycriticalcapital.com

www.myoptionvalue.com

www.mystockoptions.com

www.naspp.org

www.nceo.org

www.networthstrategies.com

www.reformAMT.org

www.stock-options.com

[*] All of these websites were operating at the time of publication (February 2003).

SAMPLE PLAN DOCUMENT

XXX, Inc.
1998 Stock Option Plan

1. <u>Purposes of the Plan.</u> The purposes of this Stock Plan are to attract and retain the best available personnel for positions of significant responsibility, to provide additional incentive for employees, directors, and consultants to continue in the long-term service of the company, and to create in such persons a more direct interest in the success of the Company's business. Options granted under the plan may be incentive stock options or nonstatutory stock options, as determined by the Administrator at the time of grant.

2. <u>Definitions.</u> As used herein, the following definitions shall apply:

   a. <u>Administrator</u> means the Board or any of its committees as shall be administering the Plan in accordance with section 4 of the Plan.

   b. <u>Affiliated Corporation</u> means any corporation or other entity that is affiliated with the Plan Sponsor through stock ownership and is designated as an "Affiliated Corporation" by the Board.

   c. <u>Applicable Laws</u> means the requirements relating to the administration of stock option plans under all applicable law, including U.S. state corporate laws, U.S. federal and state securities law, the Internal Revenue Code, any stock exchange on which the common stock is listed or quoted, and the applicable laws of any other country or jurisdiction where stock options are granted under the plan.

d. Board means the Board of Directors of the Company.

e. Code means the Internal Revenue Code of 1986, as amended.

f. Committee means a committee of Directors appointed by the Board in accordance with section 4 of the Plan and empowered to take action with respect to the administration of the Plan.

g. Common Stock means the Common Stock of the Company.

h. Company means XXX, Inc., a Delaware corporation.

i. Consultant means any person, including an advisor, engaged by the Company or any Affiliated Corporation to render services and is compensated for such services.

j. Director means a member of the Board of Directors of the Company.

k. Disability means total and permanent disability as defined in Section 22(e)(3) of the Code.

l. Employee means any person, including Officers and Directors, employed by the Company or an Affiliated Corporation. For purposes of the Plan, an Employee is an individual whose wages are subject to the withholding of federal income tax under Code 3401. A service provider shall not cease to be an Employee in the case of (i) any leave of absence approved by the company or (ii) transfers between locations of the Company. For purposes of Incentive Stock Options, no such leave may exceed 90 days, unless reemployment upon expiration of such leave is guaranteed by statute or contract. If reemployment upon expiration of a leave of absence approved by the Company is not guaranteed, on the 181st day of such leave any Incentive Stock Option held by the Optionee shall cease to be treated as an Incentive Stock Option and shall be treated for tax purposes as a Nonstatutory Stock Option. Neither service as a Director nor payment of Director's fee by the Company shall be sufficient to constitute "employment" by the Company.

m. <u>Fair Market Value</u> means the closing price of Common Stock on the principal stock exchange or automated quotation system market on which the Stock is traded for the last market trading day prior to the time of determination, as reported in *The Wall Street Journal* or such other source as the Administrator deems reliable. If the price of the Stock is not reported on any securities exchange or national market system, the Fair Market Value of the Stock shall be determined in good faith by the Administrator.

n. <u>Incentive Stock Option</u> means an Option intended to qualify as an incentive stock option in accordance with Section 422 of the Code.

o. <u>Nonstatutory Stock Option</u> means an Option not intended to qualify as an Incentive Stock Option.

p. <u>Officer</u> means a person who is an officer of the Company within the meaning of Section 16 of the Exchange Act and the rules and regulations of that Act.

q. <u>Option</u> means a right to purchase Stock at a specific price for a specific period of time. Options granted pursuant to the Plan shall be either Incentive Stock Options or Nonstatutory Stock Options.

r. <u>Option Agreement</u> means a written or electronic agreement between the Company and an Optionee stating the terms and conditions of an individual Option grant. The Option Agreement is subject to the terms and conditions of the Plan.

s. <u>Optioned Stock</u> means the Common Stock subject to an Option grant.

t. <u>Optionee or Option Holder</u> means a Participant who has been granted one or more options under the Plan.

u. <u>Option Price</u> means the grant price or strike price or exercise price; the price at which each share of Stock subject to an Option may be purchased.

v. <u>Participant</u> means an eligible employee or eligible individual designated by the Administrator to receive one or more Options under the Plan.

w. <u>Plan</u> means the XXX, Inc., 1998 Stock Option Plan.

x.   Plan Sponsor means XXX, Inc., and any successor.

y.   Share means a share of the Common Stock.

z.   Stock means the Common Stock of the Plan Sponsor.

3.   Stock Subject to the Plan. Subject to the provisions of Section 12 of the Plan, the maximum aggregate number of Shares which may be subject to option and sold under the Plan is 1,000,000 Shares. The Shares may be authorized but not yet issued or reacquired Common Stock. If an Option expires or becomes unexerciseable without having been exercised in full, the unpurchased Shares shall become available for future grant or sale under the Plan (unless the Plan is terminated). However, Shares that have actually been issued under the Plan, upon exercise of an Option, shall not be returned to the Plan and shall not become available for future distribution under the Plan.

4.   Administration of the Plan. The Plan shall be administered by the Board or a Committee appointed by the Board.

a.   Powers of the Administrator Subject to the provisions of the Plan and, in the case of a Committee, the specific duties delegated by the Board, the Administrator shall have the authority and discretion in the following areas:

i.   To determine Fair Market Value;

ii.   To select Service Providers to whom Options may be granted;

iii. To determine the number of Shares to be covered by each Option award;

iv.   To approve forms of agreement for use under the Plan;

v.   To determine the terms and conditions of any Option granted. Such terms and conditions include, but are not limited to, the exercise price, the times when Options may be exercised, any vesting acceleration or waiver of forfeiture restrictions, and any restriction or limitation regarding any Option grant;

vi.   To prescribe, amend, and rescind rules and regulations relating to the Plan;

vii. To allow Optionees to satisfy withholding tax obligations by electing to have the Company withhold from the Shares to be issued upon exercise of an Option that number of Shares having a Fair Market Value equal to the amount required to be withheld. All elections by Optionees to have Shares withheld for this purpose shall be made in such a manner as to meet the requirements determined by the Administrator.

b. Effect of Administrator's Decision. All decisions, determinations, and interpretations of the Administrator shall be final and binding on all Optionees.

5. Eligibility Nonstatutory Stock Options may be granted to Service Providers. Incentive Stock Options may be granted only to Employees.

a. Each Option shall be designated in the Option Agreement as either an Incentive Stock Option or a Nonstatutory Stock Option. However, despite such designations, the extent that the aggregate Fair Market Value of the Shares with respect to which Incentive Stock Options are exercisable for the first time by the Option holder during any single calendar year exceeds $100,000, such Options exceeding that $100,000 threshold shall be treated as Nonstatutory Stock Options. The Fair Market Value of the Shares shall be determined as of the time the Option is granted, and Incentive Stock Options shall be taken into account in the order in which they are granted for such purposes.

b. Neither the Plan nor any Option Grant shall confer upon any Service Provider any right with respect to continuing in a relationship with the Company as said Service Provider, nor shall it interfere in any way with his or her right or the Company's right to terminate such relationship and any time, with or without cause.

6. Term of the Plan. The Plan shall become effective upon its adoption by the Board. It shall continue in effect for a term of ten (10) years unless sooner terminated under Section 14 of the Plan.

7. Term of the Option. The term of each Option shall be stated in the Option Agreement and shall not be more than ten (10) years

from the date of grant. In the case of an Incentive Stock Option granted to an Optionee who, at the time the Option is granted, owns stock representing more than ten percent (10%) of the voting power of all classes of stock of the Company, the term of the Option shall be five (5) years from the date of grant.

8. Option Exercise Price and Payment.
    a. The per share price for the Shares to be issued upon exercise of an Option shall be the price determined by the Administrator, but shall be subject to the following:
        i. In the case of an Incentive Stock Option
            1. granted to an Employee only who, at the time of grant, owns stock representing more than ten percent (10%) of the voting power of all classes of Company stock, the exercise price shall be no less than 110% of the Fair Market Value per Share on the date of grant.
            2. granted to any other Employee, the per Share grant price shall be no less than 100% of the Fair Market Value per Share on the date of grant.
        ii. In the case of a Nonstatutory Stock Option
            1. granted to a Service Provider who, at the time of grant, owns stock representing more than ten percent (10%) of the voting power of all classes of Company stock, the exercise price shall be no less than 110% of the Fair Market Value per Share on the date of grant.
            2. granted to any other Service Provider, the per Share grant price shall be no less than 100% of the Fair Market Value per Share on the date of grant.
        iii. Options may be granted with a per Share exercise price other than as required above pursuant to a merger or other corporate transaction.
    b. The payment and method of payment to be made for the Shares to be issued upon exercise of an Option, shall be determined by the Administrator. Such payment may consist of (1) cash, (2) check, (3) promissory note, (4) other

Shares which have been owned by the Optionee for more than six months, (5) delivery to the Plan Sponsor of a properly executed notice of exercise together with irrevocable instructions to a broker to promptly deliver to the Plan Sponsor the amount of the proceeds of the sale of all or a portion of the Stock or of a margin loan from the broker to the Option Holder required to pay the Exercise Price, (6) any combination of the above-mentioned payment methods.

9.   Exercise of an Option

a.   Manner of Exercise. Any Option granted shall be exercisable according to the terms and conditions determined by the Administrator and set forth in the Option Agreement, but in no case at a rate of less than 25% per year over four (4) years from the date the Option is granted. Unless the Administrator provides otherwise, vesting of Options granted shall be tolled during any unpaid leave of absence. No Options may be exercised for a fraction of a Share.

An Option shall be considered exercised when the Company receives written or electronic notice of exercise (in accordance with the Option Agreement) from the person entitled to exercise the Option and full payment for the Shares, consisting of any payment and method authorized by the Administrator and permitted by the Option Agreement and Plan. Shares issued upon exercise of the Option shall be issued in the name of the Optionee or if requested by the Option Holder in the name of the Optionee and his or her spouse. The right to vote or receive dividends or any other rights of a shareholder will exist only when shares are issued.

Exercise of an Option and the corresponding issuance of Shares shall result in a decrease in the number of Shares available for the purposes of the Plan.

b.   Termination of Relationship as a Service Provider. If an Optionee ceases to be a Service Provider, the Option Holder may exercise his or her Option within a period of time specified in the Option Agreement to the extent that the Option is vested on the date of termination but not later than the expiration of the term of the Option set forth in the Option Agreement. In the absence of a specified time in the Option Agreement, the Option shall remain exercisable for ninety (90) days following the Optionee's termination. If, on the date of termination, the Option Holder is not vested, the Shares attributed to the unvested portion of the Option shall revert to the Plan. If, after termination, the Optionee does not exercise his or her Option within the time specified, the Option shall terminate and the Shares attributed to the unexercised grant will revert to the Plan.

c. <u>Disability of Option Holder.</u> If the Optionee ceases to be a Service Provider as a result of the Optionee's Disability, the Option Holder may exercise his or her Option within the period of time specified in the Option Agreement to the extent the Option is vested on the date of termination but not later than the expiration of the term of the Option set forth in the Option Agreement. In the absence of a specified time in the Option Agreement, the Option shall remain exercisable for twelve (12) months following the Optionee's termination. If on the date of termination the Optionee is not vested in his or her Option in its entirety, all unvested Shares will revert to the Plan. If, after termination, the Optionee does not exercise his or her Option within the specified time, the Option shall terminate and the Shares attributed to the unexercised grant will revert to the Plan.

d. <u>Death of an Option Holder.</u> If an Optionee dies while a Service Provider, vested Options may be exercised within the period of time specified in the Option Agreement, but not later than the expiration of the term of the Option, by the Optionee's estate or by a person who acquires the right to exercise the Option by bequest or inheritance. In the absence of a specified time in the Option Agreement, the Option shall remain exercisable for twelve (12) months following the date of death. Any Shares not vested at the time of death will revert to the Plan. The Option may be exercised by the executor or administrator of the Optionee's estate or by the person(s) entitled to exercise the Option under the Optionee's will or the laws of descent or distribution. If the Option is not exercised within the time specified, the Option shall terminate and the Shares attributed to the unexercised grant will revert to the Plan.

e. Buyout Provisions. The Administrator may at any time offer to buy out for a payment in cash or Shares an Option previously granted, based on terms and conditions the Administrator shall establish and communicate to the Optionee at the time such an offer is made.

10. Nontransferability of Options. Options may not be sold, pledged, assigned, hypothecated, transferred, or disposed of in any manner other than by will or by the laws of descent or distribution and may be exercised, during the lifetime of the Optionee, only by the Option Holder.

11. Adjustment upon Changes in Capitalization, Merger, or Asset Sale.

a. Changes in Capitalization. In the event of a stock split, reverse stock split, stock dividend, combination or reclassification of the Common Stock, the number of shares of Common Stock attributed to each outstanding Option and the number of shares of Common Stock which have been authorized for issuance under the Plan but have yet to be granted or which have been returned to the Plan upon cancellation or expiration of an Option, shall be proportionately adjusted for any increase or decrease in the number of shares of Common Stock. Such adjustment shall be made by the Board, whose determination shall be final.

b. Dissolution or Liquidation. The Administrator shall notify each Optionee as soon as possible regarding the proposed dissolution or liquidation of the Company. The Administrator in its discretion may provide for an Optionee to have the right to exercise all of his or her Options until fifteen (15) days prior to such activity, including Shares as to which the Option would not otherwise be exercisable (i.e. unvested). To the extent an Option is not exercised within the specified time period, it will terminate immediately prior to the consummation of such proposed activity.

    c.   <u>Merger or Asset Sale.</u> In the event of a merger with or into another corporation for the Company, or the sale of substantially all the assets of the Company, each outstanding Option shall be assumed or an equivalent Option substituted by the successor corporation. In the event that the successor corporation refuses to assume or substitute the Option, the Optionee shall fully vest in and have the right to exercise the Option, including Shares that would not otherwise be vested or exercisable. If an Option becomes fully vested and exercisable in the event of a merger or sale of assets, the Administrator shall notify the Optionee in writing or electronically that the Option shall be fully exercisable for a period of fifteen (15) days from the date of such notice and that the Option shall terminate upon the expiration of such period.

12.   <u>Time of Granting Options.</u> The date of grant of an Option shall be the date on which the Administrator makes the determination granting such Option. Notice of the determination shall be given to each Service Provider to whom an Option is so granted within a reasonable time after the date of such grant.

13.   <u>Amendment and Termination of the Plan.</u>

    a.   <u>Amendment and Termination.</u> The Board may at any time amend, alter, suspend, or terminate the Plan.

    b.   <u>Shareholder Approval.</u> The Board shall obtain shareholder approval of any Plan amendment to the extent necessary to comply with applicable laws.

    c.   <u>Effect of Amendment or Termination.</u> No amendment, alteration, suspension, or termination of the Plan shall impair the rights of any Option Holder, unless mutually agreed upon by the Optionee and the Administrator. Such an agreement must be in writing and signed by the Optionee and the Company. Termination of the Plan shall not affect the Administrator's ability to exercise the powers authorized with respect to the Options granted under the Plan prior to the date of such termination.

14. <u>Conditions Upon Issuance of Shares.</u>

    a.   <u>Legal Compliance.</u> Shares shall not be issued pursuant to the exercise of an Option unless the exercise of such Option and the issuance and delivery of such Shares are in compliance with applicable laws and shall be subject to the approval of counsel for the Company with respect to such compliance.

    b.   <u>Investment Representations.</u> As a condition to the exercise of an Option, the Administrator may require the person exercising the Option to represent and warrant that the Shares are being purchased only for investment and without any present intention to sell or distribute said Shares if, in the option of counsel for the Company, such a representation is required.

15. <u>Inability to Obtain Authority.</u> The inability of the Company to obtain authority from any regulatory body having jurisdiction shall relieve the Company of any liability with respect of the failure to issue or sell such Shares.

16. <u>Reservation of Shares.</u> The Company shall at all times reserve and keep available the number of Shares required to satisfy the requirements of the Plan, during the term of the Plan.

17. <u>Shareholder Approval.</u> The Plan shall be subject to the approval of the shareholders of the Company within twelve (12) months after the date the Plan is adopted.

18. <u>Information to Optionees and Purchasers.</u> The Company shall provide, at least annually, to each Optionee and to each individual who acquires Shares pursuant to the plan copies of annual financial statements. The Company shall not be required to provide such statements to key employees whose duties assure their access to equivalent information.

SAMPLE GRANT AGREEMENT

XXX, Inc.
1998 Stock Plan
Stock Option Agreement

Unless otherwise defined herein, the terms defined in the 1998 Stock Option Plan (the "Plan") shall have the same defined meanings in this Stock Option Agreement.

I. Notice of Stock Option Grant

Edward Employee
563 Central Avenue
Anytown, USA 93245

The undersigned Optionee has been granted an Option to purchase Common Stock of the Company, subject to the terms and conditions of the Plan and this Option Agreement, as follows:

Grant Number	00002345
Date of Grant	February 14, 2000
Vesting Commencement Date	02/14/2000
Exercise Price Per Share	$10.00
Total Number of Shares Granted	500
Type of Option	__X__ Incentive Stock Option
	_____ Nonstatutory Stock Option
Term/Expiration Date	February 14, 2010

Vesting Schedule

This Option shall be exercisable, in whole or in part, according to the following vesting schedule: 25% of the Shares subject to the Option shall vest on the first anniversary of the Vesting Commencement Date, and an additional 25% of the Shares subject to the Option shall vest on each of the next three anniversaries thereafter, subject to Optionee's continuing to be a Service Provider on such dates.

Termination Period

This Option shall be exercisable for three (3) months after the Optionee ceases to be a Service Provider. Upon Optionee's death or disability, this Option may be exercised for one (1) year after Optionee ceases to be a Service Provider. In no event may Optionee exercise this Option after the Term/Expiration Date as provided above.

II. Agreement

Grant of Option. The Plan Administrator of the Company hereby grants to the Optionee named in the Notice of Grant (the "Optionee") an option (the "Option") to purchase the number of Shares set forth in the Notice of Grant, at the exercise price per Share set forth in the Notice of Grant (the "Exercise Price"), and subject to the terms and conditions of the Plan, which is incorporated herein by reference. Subject to Section 13(c) of the Plan, in the event of a conflict between the terms and conditions of the Plan and this Option Agreement, the terms and conditions of the Plan shall prevail.

If designated in the Notice of Grant as an Incentive Stock Option ("ISO"), this Option is intended to qualify as an Incentive Stock Option as defined in Section 422 of the Code. Nevertheless, to the extent that it exceeds the $100,000 rule of Code Section 422(d), this Option shall be treated as a Nonstatutory Stock Option ("NSO").

Exercise of Option.

Right to Exercise. This Option shall be exercisable during its term in accordance with the Vesting Schedule set out in the Notice of

Grant and with the applicable provisions of the Plan and this Option Agreement.

Method of Exercise. This Option shall be exercisable by delivery of an exercise notice in the form attached as Exhibit A (the "Exercise Notice") which shall state the election to exercise the Option, the number of Shares with respect to which the Option is being exercised, and such other representations and agreements as may be required by the Company. The Exercise Notice shall be accompanied by payment of the aggregate Exercise Price as to all Exercised Shares. This Option shall be deemed to be exercised upon receipt by the Company of such fully executed Exercise Notice accompanied by the aggregate Exercise Price. No Shares shall be issued pursuant to the exercise of an Option unless such issuance and such exercise comply with applicable laws. Assuming such compliance, for income tax purposes the Shares shall be considered transferred to the Optionee on the date on which the Option is exercised with respect to such Shares.

Optionee's Representations. In the event the Shares have not been registered under the Securities Act of 1933, as amended, at the time this Option is exercised, the Optionee shall, if required by the Company, concurrently with the exercise of all or any portion of this Option, deliver to the Company his or her Investment Representation Statement in the form attached hereto as Exhibit B.

Lock-Up Period. Optionee hereby agrees that, if so requested by the Company or any representative of the underwriters (the "Managing Underwriter") in connection with any registration of the offering of any securities of the Company under the Securities Act, Optionee shall not sell or otherwise transfer any Shares or other securities of the Company during the 180-day period (or such other period as may be requested in writing by the Managing Underwriter and agreed to in writing by the Company) (the "Market Standoff Period") following the effective date of a registration statement of the Company filed under the Securities Act. Such restriction shall apply only to the first registration statement of the Company to become effective under the Securities Act that includes securities to be sold on behalf of the Company to the public in an underwritten public offering under the Securities Act. The Company may impose stop-transfer instructions with respect to securities subject to the foregoing restrictions until the end of such Market Standoff Period.

Method of Payment. Payment of the aggregate Exercise Price shall be by any of the following, or a combination thereof, at the election of the Optionee: (a) cash or check; (b) consideration received by the Company under a formal cashless exercise program adopted by the Company in connection with the Plan; (c) surrender of other Shares which in the case of Shares acquired upon exercise of an option, have been owned by the Optionee for more than six (6) months on the date of surrender and have a Fair Market Value on the date of surrender equal to aggregate Exercise Price of the Exercised Shares.

Restrictions on Exercise. This Option may not be exercised until such time as the Plan has been approved by the shareholders of the Company, or if the issuance of such Shares upon such exercise or the method of payment of consideration for such shares would constitute a violation of any Applicable Law.

Nontransferability of Option. This Option may not be transferred in any manner otherwise than by will or by the laws of descent and distribution and may be exercised during the lifetime of Optionee only by Optionee. The terms of the Plan and this Option Agreement shall be binding upon executors, administrators, heirs, successors, and assigns of the Optionee.

Term of Option. This Option may be exercised only within the term set out in the Notice of Grant and may be exercised during such term only in accordance with the Plan and the terms of this Option.

Tax Consequences. Set forth below is a brief summary as of the date of this Option of some of the federal tax consequences of exercise of this Option and disposition of Shares. THIS SUMMARY IS NECESSARILY INCOMPLETE, AND THE TAX LAWS AND REGULATIONS ARE SUBJECT TO CHANGE. THE OPTIONEE SHOULD CONSULT A TAX ADVISER BEFORE EXERCISING THIS OPTION OR DISPOSING OF THE SHARES.

Exercise of ISO. If this Option qualifies as an ISO, there will be no regular federal income tax liability upon the exercise of the Option, although the excess, if any, of the Fair Market Value of the Shares on the date of exercise over the Exercise Price will be treated as an adjustment to the alternative minimum tax for federal tax purposes and may subject the Optionee to the alternative minimum tax in the year of exercise.

Exercise of ISO Following Disability. If the Optionee ceases to be an Employee as a result of a disability that is not a total and permanent disability as defined in Section 22(e)(3) of the Code, to the extent permitted on the date of termination, the Optionee must exercise an ISO within three months of such termination for the ISO to be qualified as an ISO.

Exercise of Nonstatutory Stock Option. There may be a regular federal income tax liability upon the exercise of a Nonstatutory Stock Option. The Optionee will be treated as having received compensation income (taxable at ordinary income tax rates) equal to the excess, if any, of the Fair Market Value of the Shares on the date of exercise over the Exercise Price. If Optionee is an Employee or a former Employee, the Company will be required to withhold from Optionee's compensation or collect from Optionee and pay to the applicable tax authorities an amount in cash equal to a percentage of this compensation income at the time of exercise, and may refuse to honor the exercise and refuse to deliver Shares if such withholding amounts are not delivered at the time of exercise.

Disposition of Shares. In the case of an NSO, if Shares are held for at least one year, any gain realized on disposition of the Shares will be treated as long-term capital gain for federal income tax purposes. In the case of an ISO, if Shares transferred pursuant to the Option are held for at least one year after exercise and for at least two years after the Date of Grant, any gain realized on disposition of the Shares will also be treated as long-term capital gain for federal income tax purposes. If Shares purchased under an ISO are disposed of within one year after exercise or two years after the Date of Grant, any gain realized on such disposition will be treated as compensation income (taxable at ordinary income tax rates) to the extent of the difference between the Exercise Price and the lesser of (1) the Fair Market Value of the Shares on the date of exercise, or (2) the sale price of the Shares. Any additional gain will be taxed as capital gain, short-term or long-term, depending on the period that the ISO Shares were held.

Notice of Disqualifying Disposition of ISO Shares. If the Option granted to Optionee herein is an ISO, and if Optionee sells or otherwise disposes of any of the Shares acquired pursuant to the ISO on or before the later of (1) the date two years after the Date of Grant, or (2) the date one year after the date of exercise, the Optionee shall immediately notify the Company in writing of such disposition. Optionee agrees that Optionee may be subject to income tax withholding by the Company on the compensation income recognized by the Optionee.

Entire Agreement: Governing Law. The Plan is incorporated herein by reference. The Plan and this Option Agreement constitute the entire agreement of the parties with respect to the subject matter hereof and supersede in their entirety all prior undertakings and agreements of the Company and Optionee with respect to the subject matter hereof, and may not be modified adversely to the Optionee's interest except by means of a writing signed by the Company and Optionee. This agreement is governed by the internal substantive laws but not the choice of law rules of (name of state).

No Guarantee of Continued Service. OPTIONEE ACKNOWLEDGES AND AGREES THAT THE VESTING OF SHARES PURSUANT TO THE VESTING SCHEDULE HEREOF IS EARNED ONLY BY CONTINUING AS A SERVICE PROVIDER AT THE WILL OF THE COMPANY (NOT THROUGH THE ACT OF BEING HIRED, BEING GRANTED THIS OPTION, OR ACQUIRING SHARES HEREUNDER). OPTIONEE FURTHER ACKNOWLEDGES AND AGREES THAT THIS AGREEMENT, THE TRANSACTIONS CONTEMPLATED HEREUNDER, AND THE VESTING SCHEDULE SET FORTH HEREIN DO NOT CONSTITUTE AN EXPRESS OR IMPLIED PROMISE OF CONTINUED ENGAGEMENT AS A SERVICE PROVIDER FOR THE VESTING PERIOD, FOR ANY PERIOD, OR AT ALL, AND SHALL NOT INTERFERE IN ANY WAY WITH OPTIONEE'S RIGHT OR THE COMPANY'S RIGHT TO TERMINATE OPTIONEE'S RELATIONSHIP AS A SERVICE PROVIDER, WITH OR WITHOUT CAUSE.

Optionee acknowledges receipt of a copy of the Plan and represents that he or she is familiar with the terms and provisions thereof, and hereby accepts this Option subject to all of the terms and provisions thereof. Optionee has reviewed the Plan and this Option in their entirety, has had an opportunity to obtain the advice of counsel prior to executing this Option, and fully understands all provision of the Option. Optionee hereby agrees to accept as binding, conclusive, and final all decisions or interpretations of the Administrator upon any questions arising under the Plan or this Option. Optionee further agrees to notify the Company upon any change in residence address indicated below.

Optionee: XXX, Inc.

_____   _____
Signature   By

_____   _____
Print Name   Title

_____
Address

_____
City, State, Zip Code

EXHIBIT A:
EXERCISE NOTICE

1998 Stock Plan
XXX, Inc.
6547 Elm Street
Anytown, USA 94582
Attention: Secretary

1. <u>Exercise of Option.</u> Effective as of today, _____, 2_____, the undersigned ("Optionee") hereby elects to exercise Optionee's option to purchase _____ shares of the Common Stock (the "Shares") of XXX, Inc. (the "Company") under and pursuant to the 1998 Stock Plan (the "Plan") and the Stock Option Agreement dated _____, _____ (the "Option Agreement").

2. <u>Delivery of Payment.</u> Purchaser herewith delivers to the Company the full purchase price of the Shares, as set forth in the Option Agreement.

3. <u>Representations of Optionee.</u> Optionee acknowledges that Optionee has received, read and understood the Plan and the Option Agreement and agrees to abide by and be bound by their terms and conditions.

4. <u>Rights as Shareholder.</u> Until the issuance of the Shares (as evidenced by the appropriate entry on the books of the Company or of a duly authorized transfer agent of the Company), no right to vote or receive dividends or any other rights as a shareholder shall exist with respect to the Optioned Stock, notwithstanding the exercise of the Option. The Shares shall be issued to the Optionee as soon as practical after the Option is exercised. No adjustment shall be made for a dividend or

211

other right for which the record date is prior to the date of issuance except as provided in Section 12 of the Plan.

5.   Company's Right of First Refusal. Before any Shares held by Optionee or any transferee (either being sometimes referred to herein as the "Holder") may be sold or otherwise transferred (including transfer by gift or operation of law), the Company or its assignee(s) shall have a right of first refusal to purchase the Shares on the terms and conditions set forth in the Section (the "Right of First Refusal").

   a.   Notice of Proposed Transfer. The Holder of Shares shall deliver to the Company written notice (the "Notice") stating: (i) the Holder's bona fide intention to sell or otherwise transfer such Shares; (ii) the name of each proposed purchaser or other transferee ("Proposed Transferee"); (iii) the number of Shares to be transferred to each Proposed Transferee; and (iv) the bona fide cash price or other consideration for which the Holder proposes to transfer the Shares (the "Offered Price"), and the Holder shall offer the Shares at the Offered Price to the Company or its assignee(s).

   b.   Exercise of Right of First Refusal. At any time within thirty (30) days after receipt of the Notice, the Company and/or its assignee(s) may, by giving written notice to the Holder, elect to purchase all, but not less than all, of the Shares proposed to be transferred to any one or more of the Proposed Transferees, at the purchase price determined in accordance with subsection (c) below.

   c.   Purchase Price. The purchase price ("Purchase Price") for the Shares purchased by the Company or its assignee(s) under this Section shall be the Offered Price. If the Offered Price includes consideration other than cash, the cash equivalent value of the non-cash consideration shall be determined by the Board of Directors of the Company in good faith.

   d.   Payment. Payment of the Purchase Price shall be made, at the option of the Company or its assignee(s), in cash (by check), by cancellation of all or a portion of any outstanding indebtedness of the Holder to the Company (or, in the case of repurchase by an assignee, to the assignee), or by any combination thereof within 30 days after receipt of the Notice or in the manner and at the times set forth in the Notice.

e.   Holder's Right to Transfer. If all of the Shares proposed in the Notice to be transferred to a given Proposed Transferee are not purchased by the Company and/or its assignee(s) as provided in this Section, then the Holder may sell or otherwise transfer such Shares to that Proposed Transferee at the Offered price or at a higher price, provided that such sale or other transfer is consummated within 120 days after the date of the Notice, that any such sale or other transfer is effected in accordance with any applicable securities laws, and that the Proposed Transferee agrees in writing that the provisions of this Section shall continue to apply to the Shares in the hands of such Proposed Transferee. If the Shares described in the Notice are not transferred to the Proposed Transferee within such period, a new Notice shall be given to the Company, and the Company and/or its assignees shall again be offered the Right of First Refusal before any Shares held by the Holder may be sold or otherwise transferred.

f.   Exception for Certain Family Transfers. Anything to the contrary contained in this Section notwithstanding, the transfer of any or all of the Shares during the Optionee's lifetime or on the Optionee's death by will or intestacy to the Optionee's immediate family or a trust for the benefit of the Optionee's immediate family shall be exempt from the provisions of this Section. "Immediate Family" as used herein shall mean spouse, lineal descendant or antecedant, father, mother, brother or sister. In such a case, the transferee or other recipient shall receive and hold the Shares so transferred subject to the provisions of this Section, and there shall be no further transfer of such Shares except in accordance with the terms of this Section.

g.   Termination of Right of First Refusal. The Right of First Refusal shall terminate as to any Shares upon the first sale of Common Stock of the Company to the general public pursuant to a registration statement filed with and declared effective by the Securities and Exchange Commission under the Securities Act of 1933, as amended.

6.   Tax Consultation. Optionee understands that Optionee may suffer adverse tax consequences as a result of Optionee's purchase or disposition of the Shares. Optionee represents that Optionee has consulted with any tax consultants Optionee deems advisable in connection with the purchase or disposition of the Shares and that Optionee is not relying on the Company for any tax advice.

7.   Restrictive Legends and Stop-Transfer Orders.

a.   Legends. Optionee understands and agrees that the Company shall cause the legends set forth below or legends substantially equivalent thereto to be placed upon any certificate(s) evidencing ownership of the Shares together with any other legends that may be required by the Company or by state or federal securities laws:

> THE SECURITIES REPRESENTED HEREBY HAVE NOT BEEN REGISTERED UNDER THE SECURITIES ACT OF 1933 (THE "ACT") AND MAY NOT BE OFFERED, SOLD OR OTHERWISE TRANSFERRED, PLEDGED OR HYPOTHECATED UNLESS AND UNTIL REGISTERED UNDER THE ACT OR, IN THE OPINION OF COMPANY COUNSEL SATISFACTORY TO THE ISSUER OF THESE SECURITIES, SUCH OFFER, SALE OR TRANSFER, PLEDGE OR HYPOTHECATION IS IN COMPLIANCE THEREWITH.

> THE SHARES REPRESENTED BY THIS CERTIFICATE ARE SUBJECT TO CERTAIN RESTRICTIONS ON TRANSFER AND A RIGHT OF FIRST REFUSAL HELD BY THE ISSUER OR ITS ASSIGNEE(S) AS SET FORTH IN THE EXERCISE NOTICE BETWEEN THE ISSUER AND THE ORIGINAL HOLDER OF THESE SHARES, A COPY OF WHICH MAY BE OBTAINED AT THE

PRINCIPAL OFFICE OF THE ISSUER. SUCH TRANS-
FER RESTRICTIONS AND RIGHT OF FIRST REFUSAL
ARE BINDING ON TRANFEREES OF THESE SHARES.

b.   Stop-Transfer Notices. Optionee agrees that, in order to ensure compliance with the restrictions referred to herein, the Company may issue appropriate "stop transfer" instructions to its transfer agent, if any, and that, if the Company transfers its own securities, it may make appropriate notations to the same effect in its own records.

c.   Refusal to Transfer. The Company shall not be required (i) to transfer on its books any Shares that have been sold or otherwise transferred in violation of any of the provisions of this Agreement or (ii) to treat as owner of such Shares or to accord the right to vote of pay dividends to any purchaser or other transferee to whom such Shares shall have been so transferred.

8. Successors and Assigns. The Company may assign any of its rights under this Agreement to single or multiple assignees, and this Agreement shall inure to the benefit of the successors and assigns of the Company. Subject to the restrictions on transfer herein set forth, this Agreement shall be binding upon Optionee and his or her heirs, executors, administrators, successors and assigns.

9. Interpretation. Any dispute regarding the interpretation of this Agreement shall be submitted by Optionee or by the Company forthwith to the Administrator, which shall review such dispute at its next regular meeting. The resolution of such a dispute by the Administrator shall be final and binding on all parties.

10. Governing Law: Severablility. This Agreement is governed by the internal substantive laws but not the choice of law rules of (name of state).

11. Entire Agreement. The Plan and Option Agreement are incorporated herein by reference. This Agreement, the Plan, the Option Agreement, and the Investment Representation Statement constitute the entire agreement of the parties with respect to the subject matter hereof and supersede in their entirety all prior undertakings and agreements of the Company and Op-

tionee with respect to the subject matter hereof, and may not be modified adversely to the Optionee's interest except by means of a writing signed by the Company and Optionee.

Submitted by: Accepted by:

Optionee   XXX, Inc.

_____   _____
Signature   By

_____   _____
Print Name   Title

_____   _____
Address   Address

_____   _____
City, State, Zip Code   City, State, Zip Code

                                           _____
                                           Date Received

EXHIBIT B: INVESTMENT REPRESENTATION STATEMENT

Optionee:
Company: XXX, Inc.
Security: Common Stock
Amount:
Date:

In connection with the purchase of the above-listed Securities, the undersigned Optionee represents to the Company the following:

a.   Optionee is aware of the Company's business affairs and financial condition and has acquired sufficient information about the Company to reach an informed and knowledgeable decision to acquire the Securities. Optionee is acquiring these Securities for investment for Optionee's own account only and not with a view to, or for resale in connection with, any "distribution" thereof within the meaning of the Securities Act of 1933, as amended (the "Securities Act").

b.   Optionee acknowledges and understands that the Securities constitute "restricted securities" under the Securities Act and have not been registered under the Securities Act in reliance upon a specific exemption therefrom, which exemption depends upon, among other things, the bona fide nature of Optionee's investment intent as expressed herein. In this connection, Optionee understands that, in the view of the Securities and Exchange Commission, the statutory basis for such exemption may be unavailable if Optionee's representation was predicated solely upon a present intention to hold these Securities for the minimum capital gains period specified under tax statutes, for a deferred sale, for or until an increase or decrease in the market price of the Securities, or for a period of one year or any other fixed period in the future. Optionee further understands that the Securities must be held indefinitely unless they are subsequently registered under the Securities Act or an exemption from such registration is available. Optionee further acknowledges and understands that the Company is under no obligation to register the Securities. Optionee understands that the certificate evidencing the Securities will be imprinted with a legend which prohibits the transfer of the Securities unless they are registered or such registration is not required in the opinion of counsel satisfactory to the Company, a legend prohibiting their transfer without the consent of the Commissioner of Corporations of the State of _____ and any other legend required under applicable state securities laws.

c.   Optionee is familiar with the provisions of Rule 701 and Rule 144, each promulgated under Securities Act, which, in substance, permit limited public resale of "restricted securities" acquired, directly or indirectly from the issuer thereof, in a nonpublic offering subject to the satisfaction of certain conditions. Rule 701 provides that if the issuer qualifies under Rule 701 at the time of the grant of the Option to the Optionee, the exercise will be exempt from registration under the Securities Act. In the event the Company becomes subject to the reporting requirements of Section 13 or 15(d) of the Securities Exchange Act of 1934, ninety (90) days thereafter (or such longer period as any market stand-off agreement may require) the Securities exempt under Rule 701 may be resold, subject to the satisfaction of certain of the conditions specified by Rule 144, including: (1) the resale being made through a broker in an unsolicited "broker's transaction" or in transactions directly with a market maker (as said term is defined under the Securities Exchange Act of 1934); and, in the case of an affiliate, (2) the availability of certain public information about the Company, (3) the amount of Securities being sold during any three month period not exceeding the limitations specified in Rule 144(e), and (4) the timely filing of a Form 144, if applicable.

In the event that the Company does not qualify under Rule 701 at the time of grant of the Option, then the Securities may be resold in certain limited circumstances subject to the provisions of Rule 144, which requires the resale to occur not less than two (2) years after the later of the date the Securities were sold by the Company or the date the Securities were sold by an affiliate of the Company, within the meaning of Rule 144; and, in case of acquisition of the Securities by an affiliate, or by a non-affiliate who subsequently holds the Securities less than three (3) years, the satisfaction of the conditions set forth in sections (1), (2), (3), and (4) of the paragraph immediately above.

d. Optionee further understands that in the event all of the applicable requirements of Rule 701 or 144 are not satisfied, registration under the Securities Act, compliance with Regulation A, or some other registration exemption will be required; and that, notwithstanding the fact that Rules 144 and 701 are not exclusive, the Staff of the Securities and Exchange Commission has expressed its opinion that persons proposing to sell private placement other than in a registered offering and otherwise than pursuant to Rules 144 or 701 will have a substantial burden of proof in establishing that an exemption from registration is available for such offers or sales, and that such persons and their respective brokers who participate in such transactions do so at their own risk. Optionee understands that no assurances can be given that any such other registration exemption will be available in such event.

Signature of Optionee:

_____

_____

Date

83(B) Election Statement

Taxpayer name: _____
Social Security Number: _____
Address: _____
Property for which the election is made: _____
Date on which the property was transferred: _____
Taxable year in which the election is made: _____
Restrictions to which the property is subject: _____
Fair Market Value on date of election: _____
Amount paid for the property: _____
Taxable Spread [*] _____

I have provided copies of this statement as required under the regulations for Section 83.

Dated this the _____ day of _____, 20___.

_____
Your Signature

[*](Fair Market Value minus Amount Paid for the property)

SAMPLE INVESTMENT POLICY STATEMENT

Presented by
a Registered Investment Adviser

Investment Policy Statement and Summary
for
(Client Name Here)

This Investment Policy Statement sets out the general guidelines, assumptions, and mutual understandings you and we have about your expectations and the investment of your portfolio. This is a working document and must be an accurate reflection of you and your needs. Whenever your needs or circumstances change, it should be reviewed and, if necessary, rewritten to ensure that it remains current and reflects your situation. Its goal is to see that your portfolio is invested to give you the mix of Safety, Income, Growth, Liquidity, and Tax Benefits you need to meet your objectives.

Personal Considerations

The Key Objective of the Portfolio.

The most important objective of this portfolio is…(insert your priorities here)

Example: Achieve financial independence by age 55, allowing you to maintain your current lifestyle without your current employment.

When we are reviewing your investment planning three years from now, it must have

_____

for you to feel that your most important goals are being met.

Projected Cash Flow Needs.

Example: No cash withdrawals are anticipated until financial independence.

Anticipated Additional Investments.

Example: Additional monthly cash investments are expected in an amount to equal $10,000 per year until financial independence. This funding will come from excess cash flow and is in addition to your participation in qualified retirement plans.

Risk Considerations.

You understand that the following risks exist and that every investment portfolio will be a balance between some or all of them: Inflation Risk—The greatest long-term risk to your financial security is your loss of purchasing power due to inflation. For example, at only 3% annual inflation, in 10 years you lose over 26% of your purchasing power and in 20 years nearly 50%.

Interest Rate Risk—This is the fluctuation in value that occurs when interest rates change. If interest rates go up, the market value of interest sensitive investments will go down; when interest rates go down, income or cash flow may be reduced.

Reinvestment Risk—This is the risk that the principal from a maturing, interest paying investment such as a certificate of deposit, a deferred fixed annuity, or an individual bond cannot be reinvested to generate the same level of income as before. This has been a significant risk since the early 1980s as interest rates have generally fallen.

Market Risk—The day-to-day fluctuations in value that always occur in every investment market. In some markets the fluctuations can be very severe, especially over the short term. This is a short-term risk, but often one of the most difficult to experience.

Non-Diversification Risk—A nondiversified portfolio will fluctuate more in market value than a properly diversified portfolio. Thus, for any given level of investment return, a nondiversified portfolio is riskier than a diversified portfolio.

Timing Risk—Although a portfolio may earn its expected rate of return over the long term, there is the risk that the pattern or timing of the returns actually earned will work against you. For an extreme example, a two-year investment result of –100% and +100% has an average return of 0%. However, after the first year, there would be nothing left. To minimize Timing Risk a number of different patterns of returns should be analyzed to determine the percentage of times a given portfolio is likely to succeed.

Investor Behavior—The past 10–15 years of very strong investment markets have brought another risk into focus —the risk of investor behavior. Many studies have shown that the average investor's investment returns are substantially below the investment returns of the markets in which they have invested. In other words, the investments they have made have done well, but they, as investors have not. This happens because they attempt to time the markets, act as a short-term investor, and fail to have and stick to a well-developed investment plan.

Acceptable Annual Fluctuation in Value—Although proper diversification through using asset allocation techniques can reduce the chance of negative returns, only an ultraconservative portfolio invested primarily in Safety of Principal investments can guarantee no nominal losses. However, an ultraconservative portfolio will usually have a negative real return because of inflation. Any portfolio using investments such as bonds or stocks will always have some fluctuation in market value.

Risk/Return Expectations.

Target Minimum Return—In order to meet your goals you want to achieve a minimum average annual return of ___% over a (short/ long) time horizon.

OR

The Focus Is to Be on Risk Management—You want your core portfolio to consist of investments that have historically taken Average / Below Average Risks while achieving Average / Above Average Returns when compared to investments with similar objectives. This is to be determined from information provided by independent third parties such as Morningstar, Lipper, Standard and Poors, etc.

This also means that when a choice is being made between two similar investments, you want the selection bias to favor the lower volatility investment instead of the investment with the higher potential return.

OR

The Focus Is to Be on Higher Returns—You want your core portfolio to consist of investments that have historically sought and achieved Above Average to High Returns. In seeking higher returns you are willing to take Above Average Risks when compared to investments with similar objectives. This is to be determined from information provided by independent third parties such as Morningstar, Lipper, Standard and Poors, etc.

This also means that when a choice is being made between two similar investments, you want the selection bias to favor the investment with the higher potential return instead of the investment with lower volatility or risk.

Management

There is no such thing as a standard portfolio. Portfolio management is the art and science of building and managing a portfolio that gives you the best chance of meeting your personal goals. Once you determine those goals, the portfolio should be managed to achieve them, and its success or failure measured by whether or not you meet those goals.

Investment Goal.

In order to meet your goals your investments must (SELECT ONE) maintain the value of your original principal / produce current income plus sufficient growth to offset inflation / produce current income plus moderate growth in excess of inflation / provide a balance of growth and income / seek growth while providing moderate income / provide long-term growth / achieve maximum growth in value.

Therefore, your investments should (SELECT ONE) provide Principal Stability / Current Income / Current Income with Moderate Growth / Growth and Income / Growth with Moderate Income / Growth / Aggressive Growth.

Investment Time Horizon.

Planning will be based on (SELECT ONE) a Short (less than 4 years) / Intermediate (4 to 10 years) / Long (10 years or more) investment time horizon.

This is being used for your planning because (INSERT A REASON SUCH AS "you will need to change your portfolio from a growth portfolio to an income portfolio in ___ years.")

Key Assumptions.

Inflation Environment—We are assuming that inflation will be (SELECT ONE) Low to Moderate to High to Very High over the period of your investment time horizon.

Interest Rates—We are assuming that interest rates will be (SELECT ONE) Falling Rapidly / Decreasing Somewhat / Relatively

Flat to Increasing Somewhat / Increasing Significantly in the next 1–2 years.

Threat to Financial Security—The greatest threat to your long-term financial independence is (SELECT ONE) inflation / loss of principal / failure to regularly add to your portfolio / the failure to follow your long-term investment plan / the risk that the timing or pattern of the investment returns you actually achieve will deplete your capital too early / _____.

Unique Portfolio Requirements.

If there are any special requirements, state them. For example, "Although this portfolio is a long-term investment, you need to withdraw $100,000/year in 1997 and 1998 to pay off a note that is due at that time."

Investment Selection Criteria.

The portfolio may consist of two broad groups, a Core Portfolio and a more Specialized one.

The Core Portfolio should consist of investments that are broad in scope and widely diversified among different types of investments and sectors.

The Specialized Portfolio would be more narrowly focused or specialized. It would invest in REITs, precious metals, natural resources, sector funds, or other investments that may not be highly diversified.

Core Portfolio—Unless you have specifically chosen to seek higher returns by using higher-risk investments, the investments selected for the core portfolio should have average or above average risk-adjusted returns achieved while taking average or below average risk.

Equity investments in the Core Portfolio should generally be balanced between Value-style investments and Growth-style investments.

<u>Specialized Portfolio</u>—Whenever possible, specialized investments should also meet the same criteria as the Core Portfolio. However, you understand that some narrowly focused products may not be able to meet this criteria.

Investment Techniques to Consider.

We may use the following investment techniques when appropriate: (SELECT AS DESIRED)

Lump Sum Investing
  Immediately investing your funds in a diversified portfolio.
Dollar-Cost Averaging
  The regular, periodic investment of your funds from current income, a cash account, or a low-volatility fixed income account into a diversified portfolio.
Lump Sum and Dollar-Cost Averaging in Combination
  Immediately investing a portion of your funds in a diversified portfolio and investing the balance by making a regular, periodic transfer of your funds from a cash account or a low-volatility fixed-income account into the diversified portfolio.
Split Annuities / Guaranteed and Variable
  Splitting your investments between a tax-deferred annuity that is guaranteed to return your original total principal by a specified date <u>and</u> variable investments, either mutual funds or variable annuities, to provide growth.
Split Annuities / Immediate and Deferred
  Splitting your investments between an immediate annuity to provide you with immediate income for a fixed period of time <u>and</u> a deferred annuity to create a pool of funds that will be available to you when payments from the immediate annuity stop.
Laddering the Maturities of Fixed-Income Investments
  Structuring the Debt Income portion of your portfolio with investments of different average durations or maturities in order to diversify the interest rate risk.

Cross-Investing
   Directing the dividends or interest from some investments into
   another investment. This is a form of dollar-cost averaging.

Systematic Withdrawal Plans
   Investing in mutual funds, variable annuities, or similar investments and arranging for a periodic check for a predetermined
   amount to be sent to you. This provides for a very predictable
   income stream and allows you to receive cash flow from more
   growth-oriented investments.

Asset Allocation

Numerous studies have shown that how you allocate your investments among the major asset classes has the greatest impact on the
returns you will earn and risks you will take. The asset allocation
decision is an extremely important factor in determining your investment results. For these reasons, the asset allocation decisions that
are made will have a major impact on the long-term results of your
portfolio.

Asset Constraints.

Current Assets That Must Be Retained:
   List any current investment asset that they won't or can't sell
   for any reason (no market, tied in with other owners, emotional
   ties, heavy capital gains exposure, it's both an investment and
   a personal asset like a mountain cabin, etc.). It's best to state the
   asset and the reason.

Current Assets That Cannot Be Divided:
   Any current investment asset that has to be kept whole or sold
   in its entirety, such as a major piece of real estate.

Assets to Ignore in the Allocation Process:
   Any current investment asset that you can treat as nonexistent
   when you do your allocations. Usually the reason is that it is
   such a large percentage of the portfolio that it distorts any
   reasonable allocation. This might also include limited partnerships.

Investments to Be Avoided:

Anything the client won't buy or you won't sell, such as limited partnerships, individual securities, etc. A useful phrase is: Limited partnerships, private issues, and individual securities about which you do not have direct, personal and expert knowledge.

Portfolio Design and Asset Allocation.

	Nondiversified	Diversified
Concentrated	Few Stocks, Single Sector, Single Asset Class/Style, or Theme	A Number of Stocks, a Few Sectors, Closely Related Classes, or Theme
Asset Allocation	Full Asset Allocation but Fewer Holdings, Little or no Style Diversification, or Narrow Themes	Full Asset Allocation with Numerous Holdings, Diversified by Style, and Broad Themes

You want your portfolio to be allocated and managed as a concentrated, nondiversified, concentrated, diversified, asset allocated but nondiversified, asset allocated and diversified portfolio.

Your recommended portfolio design and asset allocation will be described in detail in a separate Design Supplement.

Income Tax Planning

Taxes can be a severe drag on investors' ability to meet their financial objectives. Over the past 20 years the typical balanced portfolio has lost almost 50% of its pretax accumulated value to income taxes. Therefore, to the extent your portfolio is subject to current income taxes, your planning should use appropriate strategies to minimize those taxes.

Income Tax Considerations.

Because your portfolio is/is not significantly exposed to current income taxes, (SELECT ONE) maximum efforts shall be made to eliminate or defer income taxes consistent with prudent economic planning.

wherever it is reasonable to do so, tax-free or tax-deferred investments should be used.

income tax planning is not a consideration for this plan.

Fees and Expenses

Inappropriate expenses can be a real drag on portfolio performance. It's important to understand what you are paying and what you are getting for your money.

The costs must be appropriate for the quality of benefits and services you receive. Fees and Expenses fall into four broad categories:

Investment Management Fees—Those fees paid for the day-to-day management of the portfolio by the portfolio managers. These costs may range from 20 to 100 basis points (0.20% to 1.00%) or more depending on the type of account, the manager, and the number of additional services that may be included.

Trading and Other Operational Expenses—The costs associated with buying and selling investments. These may include transaction fees, transfer and custodial fees, markups and markdowns. Excluding markups and markdowns, these expenses typically range between 25 and 250 basis points (0.25% to 2.50%) per year depending on the type of account, its turnover, etc.

Administration Expenses—In addition to those fees charged directly for investment management and operations, there may be expenses for other services, including independent reporting and monitoring, manager due diligence, and account servicing.

Advisory Fees—These fees pay for ongoing advice. Because the other fees do not pay for services that are specific and unique to you, advisory services are the critical link between you, the investment manager and the day-to-day operation of the portfolio.

For this portfolio your total fees, including all of the above services, are estimated to be about ___% per year of the value of your managed accounts.

Reporting and Accountability

Once your portfolio is up and running, you need procedures in place to monitor where it's going and whether or not you are likely to end up where you want to be. Ultimately the success or failure of your investments will be determined by how closely they allow you to achieve your goals.

Reporting Requirements.

A statement reflecting the investments we have handled for you will be prepared and mailed to you (SELECT ONE) monthly / quarterly / semi-annually / annually.

A portfolio performance summary reflecting the investments we have handled for you will be prepared and mailed to you quarterly.

(OPTIONAL) Near the end of the implementation period when your accounts have been set up and the initial investments are being made, we should plan on meeting to review what has been done and what remains to be done to complete the first phase of your investment planning.

Periodic Reviews.

In addition to the periodic reports you receive, we should meet periodically to review your objectives and your portfolio. Initially we should plan on meeting every 3/4/6/12 months.

(OPTIONAL if using Monte Carlo simulations)

Once a year we should update the asset allocation simulations we have done to ensure that your asset allocation continues to give you the probability of successfully meeting your goals that you want.

Our first review meeting should be in _____.

Portfolio Rebalancing.

Your asset allocation should be monitored regularly and rebalanced periodically. In most cases this will not have to be done more often than once a year unless there are substantial movements in the value of one asset class or substantial withdrawals are made.

In addition, if a change in your circumstances or a basic change in the assumptions underlying your asset allocation occurs, it may be necessary to recommend a change in the asset allocation of your portfolio.

Monitoring and Managing the Managers.

Once appropriate managers and investments are selected you want to be patient and allow the managers sufficient time to manage the portions of the portfolios allocated to them through at least a full market cycle / the managers monitored closely and replaced at any sign of long-term weakness.

Changes in Objectives.

In the event your needs, objectives, risk tolerance or circumstances change, this Investment Policy Statement should be reviewed, revised if necessary and your portfolio adjusted accordingly. Please contact us immediately if changes occur.

Client _____ Date _____

Client _____ Date _____

Investment Adviser Representative
_____ Date _____

Source: Private Advisory Group, LLC.

BEGINNING THE OPTIONEERING® PROCESS

If you would like some assistance in locating professionals you can work with to begin the Optioneering® process, you can contact us for assistance:

Beth V. Walker
Private Advisory Group, LLC.
1120 N. Town Center Drive, Suite 160
Las Vegas, NV 89144
ph. (702) 341-1170
fax (702) 341-1176
beth@optioneering.net
www.pagplan.com

Index